The Horse Listener

By Mark M. Hanna

For a millennia
I have loved you
With faith as my guide
For promises fulfilled
I have anxiously waited

Mark M. Hanna

Published by Best Seller Publishing®, Pasadena, CA
Best Seller Publishing® is a registered trademark
Printed in the United States of America.
ISBN: 978-1-946978-70-7

This publication is designed to provide accurate and authoritative information with regard to the subject matter covered. It is sold with the understanding that the publisher is not engaged in rendering legal, accounting, or other professional advice. If legal advice or other expert assistance is required, the services of a competent professional should be sought. The opinions expressed by the authors in this book are not endorsed by Best Seller Publishing® and are the sole responsibility of the author rendering the opinion.

Most Best Seller Publishing® titles are available at special quantity discounts for bulk purchases for sales promotions, premiums, fundraising, and educational use. Special versions or book excerpts can also be created to fit specific needs.

For more information, please write:
Best Seller Publishing®
1346 Walnut Street, #205
Pasadena, CA 91106
or call 1(626) 765 9750
Toll Free: 1(844) 850-3500

Visit us online at: www.BestSellerPublishing.org

Table of Contents

Dedication vii

Foreword ix

Preface xi

Prologue xiii

Introduction 1

Chapter 1: Miracle of Birth 5

Chapter 2: The Horse Bug 7

Chapter 3: A Horse in the Barn 11

Chapter 4: The Trucker Across the Street 13

Chapter 5: My Majestic Princess 21

Chapter 6: The New Foal 27

Chapter 7: The Grange Hall 29

Chapter 8: Who Is Mike Chapman? 33

Chapter 9: Mike's Depression 37

Chapter 10: You Know Me Too Well 41

Chapter 11: A Little Horse Therapy 43

Chapter 12: Mike's Passion Rekindled 45

Chapter 13: Momma and Baby 49

Chapter 14: The Nature of Horses 53

Chapter 15: A Playday I'll Never Forget 57

Chapter 16: A Mother's Love 65

Chapter 17: Mike's Overdue Visit 67

Chapter 18: That Squirrelly A Rab 71

Chapter 19: Mike's Epiphany 77

Chapter 20: Shahwan 85

Chapter 21: My First Riding Lesson 93

Chapter 22: A Valuable Lesson 95

Chapter 23: Fond Memories...99

Chapter 24: Plans for Mike 101

Chapter 25: Miya's Forgiveness.. 107

Chapter 26: Marcia's Secret 113

Chapter 27: A Little White Lie 117

Chapter 28: Mike's Big Surprise 121

Chapter 29: Mike's Unexpected Gift 127

Chapter 30: Shahwanyssa, The Wild One 133

Chapter 31: Sissy, Our Spirited Filly...................................... 135

Chapter 32: Fighting Our Nature... 141

Chapter 33: Shirley's Amazement... 151

Chapter 34: Horse Listener 157

Chapter 35: Mike's Spirit Guides 161

Chapter 36: College Bound.. 165

Chapter 37: Change on the Horizon 175

Chapter 38: An Offer Mike Can't Refuse 181

Chapter 39: A Growing Family 189

Chapter 40: Mike's Unexpected Adventure 197

Chapter 41: Mike's Safe Return... 209

Chapter 42: Shahwan's Legacy 211

Chapter 43: Saving a Bloodline 213

Dedication

Throughout my lifetime, I have come to the strong belief and testimony that a Creator greater than me had a hand in all our experiences: those that have come before and those that have yet to transpire. The wise Fatherly counsel would have a hand in guiding me from across the veil. Not only because of faith but by experiences garnered during my existence here on this earth have I come to this strong belief. This amazing earth we live on, with all of its creation, is awe-inspiring.

I dedicate this work first to my heavenly Father (my Creator) for giving me the opportunity to share in his creation.

To the horse, especially the Arabian horse.

To the many masters who have come before me who have committed their lives to understanding and perfecting our relationship with the horse. Mankind has expanded their ability to populate this world because of the horse.

To my many mentors, especially Frederic Pignon and Magali Delgado, who have guided me through my learning and understanding of the horse.

To my mother who supported me throughout, unceasingly.

To my late friend Walter Heuser and his wife Margit who led me to my soul mate.

To the legacy of my soul mate *Shahwan GASB, an Arabian stallion who will live forever in my soul, and all his future offspring.

To the future horsemen and horsewomen who will apply the lessons herein, and to the legacy of the devoted equestrians that will result.

Foreword

By Linda Brown, Prairie Gem Stables, Omaha, Nebraska. Jubilee Horse Rescue.

In the world of horse breeding, whether the plan for the horse is competition or pleasure, animal welfare is of the highest consideration for the horse owner. Knowing Mark Hanna for many years, I have seen him work with his own horses, as well as other people's horses, and he continues to amaze me with his gentle effective handling, which achieves a level of trust and willingness that benefits the handler as well as the horse.

Mark's passion to preserve the natural personality and happiness of the Arabian horses is definitely portrayed in this book, along with a vast amount of history of the origin of the Arabian horse with a continued journey through the generations of breeding these fine horses.

While reading Mark's book, I felt like I was watching a movie and didn't want the book to end. Mark takes the reader through a young man's life growing up with horses, entwining the value of horse and human relationships. Determination, patience, the desire to learn, honesty, trust, and perseverance are truly portrayed in an easy to understand collection of valuable lessons of life for young as well as mature readers, whether the reader is a rider, owner, or just an admirer of horses, or someone interested in the history of the Arabian.

This book places highly the importance of family, a personal closeness to God, overcoming obstacles that hinder life's success, and it addresses the wonderful nature, athleticism and beauty of the Arabian horse. This book sheds a wonderful light of understanding upon the never-ending pursuit of happiness with the assistance of loving equines.

Preface

I was not unlike many other young boys or girls who were infatuated by and dreamed about the horse. From my suburban home in Inglewood, California, the adjacent Hollywood Park Race Track beckoned me, and I could hear the starting bells, the cheering crowds, and the pounding hooves from my bedroom.

At the time, the world of horses was only accessed by my imagination and the book *The Black Stallion*. My youthful exuberance towards horses finally convinced my big sister to take me to the morning workouts at the track, where the strangely familiar smells and ambiance of the horses emerging through the morning fog on the track convinced me that horses would dominate my life.

I was an angry young man after losing my father at the age of six. My second name rhymed with banana and I had very curly hair, so I was relentlessly teased. The only way I could cope with these conditions was to overcompensate with every aspect of my life. My athletics became my way out. I was a very clumsy youth but with my brother's help developed into a strong dominating competitor. Even with this compensation, I still experienced the teasing.

I became a very controlling person. I had been taught by my mother to be a caring, kind and courageous person who was not afraid to be true to myself. Even with this instilled motivation, my anger and controlling nature would affect my dealings with the love of my life, the Arabian horse.

My dreams came true with the building of my own Arabian horse ranch that was populated with the precious horses I dreamed about so often in the books by Walter Farley. I realized, after many years of following the Arabian horse across the country, that my anger was my downfall. I followed a dominating form of training that included intimidation and fear to elicit the beautiful movement and attractive traits that the Arabian horse was known for. After my beloved young stallion, during a training session reached out and bit me savagely, I realized what I was doing to my horses that I loved so much. I experienced an epiphany after that experience that launched me onto a path180 degrees from the submission I sought from my horses. I immediately understood the innate small voice I heard since my youth to be kind, have courage and be true to myself. I was fighting against and ignoring this counsel to my disadvantage. There was another way to achieve a horse's cooperation without force or submission. I embarked on a search for the answer. My belief in a Divine Creator God and the mentorship of influential horsemen throughout the world has led me to an understanding that there is another path to follow when becoming a partner with your horse.

There is a message of redemption for souls who have lost their way. Get up when you fall and never give up. Never fail to follow your dreams. Failure is just a step on the path. The "realist" sees his path, the "dreamer" has already been there on that path.

I want to attribute to my Soulmate, the Arabian stallion *Shahwan GASB, also my good friend Darik Anderson who helped change my life, the strong and gentle character they exhibited that beckoned me on a journey toward becoming a "Horse Listener". For a horse whispers to us and we become the listener. And to my mentors Frederic Pignon and Magali Delgado, the co-founders of Cavalia who are, in my opinion, the finest and most sensitive horse people in the world.

My motivation in writing this book, a fictional autobiography based on true life events, is based upon my desire to help change the culture of force and submission that exists to the detriment of our horses. My desire is to guide the youth and new horseman in the world to embark on a path different to mine when starting a life with the horse of their dreams, especially the majestic Arabian horse.

Prologue

It is believed that perception is reality. I'm here to tell you, that is not always the case. My name is Mathew Peters. I was just a typical uprooted big city kid, living with my recently widowed mother, wondering how I'd survive the scary transition to the high desert of Central Oregon, from the city lights to absolute darkness.

You may be wondering. What does this have to do with horses? Patience. I'll get to that eventually. Some might call this a love story about a man and his horse. How can a horse help us?

You never know how far someone has come and what they have learned or lost along the way. You meet someone who is an enigma at first, who rocks your world and guides you into what seems like an alternate universe of the horse, where the horse whispers in your ear, and you become the listener.

God creates our world, gives us free will, and sends our souls here to inhabit bodies both animal and human. We think we have it all figured out, with such high expectations. This world is a cruel world after all. What if you could relive your life through someone else? Of course you can't, but you can help someone else avoid your mistakes.

Promises made in the pre-existence are hard to keep when you cross the veil to live in this difficult world. Our Creator gave us counsel before we lost our memory of our premortal existence. Some of us have an innate knowledge of this advice and strive to follow that still small voice, but some ignore it all together.

Introduction

From the King James Bible:

Genesis, Chapter 1

1. In the beginning God created the heaven and the earth.

24. And God said, Let the earth bring forth the living creature after his kind, cattle, and creeping thing, and beast of the earth after his kind: and it was so.

25. And God made the beast of the earth after his kind, and cattle after their kind, and everything that creepeth upon the earth after his kind: and God saw that it was good.

26. And God said; Let us make man in our image, after our likeness: and let them have dominion over the fish of the sea, and over the fowl of the air, and over the cattle, and over all the earth, and over every creeping thing that creepeth upon the earth.

27. So God created man in his own image, in the image of God created he him; male and female created he them.

28. And God blessed them, and God said unto them, be fruitful, and multiply, and replenish the earth, and subdue it: and have dominion over the fish of the sea, and over the fowl of the air, and over every living thing that moveth upon the earth.

Genesis, Chapter 2

18. And the LORD God said, it is not good that the man should be alone; I will make him an help meet for him.

19. And out of the ground the LORD God formed every beast of the field, and every fowl of the air; and brought them unto Adam to see what he would call them: and whatsoever Adam called every living creature, that was the name thereof.

20. And Adam gave names to all cattle, and to the fowl of the air, and to every beast of the field.

When all this was accomplished, God said that it was good. He called together a grand council of all spirits and said, "See what I have done for you. I have created the heaven and the earth, but I give you this counsel; I love you, my children. With great favor, I have created this beautiful world for your habitation. When you leave here and enter the unique bodies I have created for you, you will have no memory of what went before. Keep this counsel at all times. Follow the plan of happiness. Have courage. Be kind. Have faith and stay true to yourself."

There was joy among God's creations, a feeling of excitement and anticipation for what was to come. The myriad of spirits present gathered together. Man and beast formed kindred groups.

"God, our Master, has given us these wonderful spirits, where before there was only an intelligence. I am now a being of spirit," said one to another. "I seem to have knowledge about you, my fellow spirits. We should get together and form families and promise each other that we will be together on earth. Look, you are different than me. Isn't that interesting? You have four legs, and I have only two legs," continued the man.

"Yes indeed, I do have four legs and I'm called horse. Adam gave me that name," the horse answered.

"You, little one, have four legs but what are you?" the man asked.

"I'm a dog," said one, and "I'm a cat," another said.

"This is great," exclaimed the man. Look, there are so many beautiful spirits, but they're so different. It has been made known to us by our Master that neither of us will be better than the next. We have an important role in the future, armed with the important counsel that God, our Master, has given us in our new creation called the earth."

There was much excitement as we anticipated our departure. The two-legged humans gathered together their families. They decided to go down together. Even the four-legged creatures made pacts with the humans to join them. There were two spirits, one two-legged and the other four-legged, that came together and made a pact to find each other, once on earth. Their bond was very strong, soulmates as they were called. Little did they know that what they thought they could accomplish together was going to be a very difficult mission!

Once they were on the other side of the veil between heaven and earth, their memory was taken from them. Even though the Master told everyone that through their choices, the promises made in heaven would be hard to keep, His spirit would always be with them. Many lifetimes came and went. There were two kindred spirits that had a hard time keeping their promises to stay together. They would pass in the world many times until they found each other. That was such for everyone. We strived to make our commitments good. Some people with their animals didn't follow the counsel given them by God in heaven, and they suffered at each other's hands. This impression was very strong in some creatures, and they remembered and strived to make the world a better place for each other.

CHAPTER 1

Miracle of Birth

The big, beautiful, gray Arabian mare circled in her stall; her waters had already broken. She had lain down once already to position the foal. Her contractions were closer together now. She lay down again and started that one big push. There's the amnion followed by one foot and then the nose. She sat up nervously looking around as another contraction pushed the second little foot out. Then push, push again until that which had been inside her was emerging with the tongue sticking out all blue. The pushes became harder. Then she got up, moved around more, and lay back down. Then the final big push came with the appearance of the baby's shoulder, and finally, the foal slipped out with a big splash.

The foal took a big gasp of air for the first time. The mare lay there panting, out of breath. Resting, the foal began breathing regularly now. As both mother and newborn son rested, Mom sat up, looked around, and saw the little body that just emerged from her, thrashing around a little bit, making movement, massaging his lungs for the first time, the umbilical cord attached pumping that final blood into his body. A soft nicker came from Mom as she instinctively recognized that smell, the amniotic fluid, which so long protected her baby, was wafting through the air. The baby was struggling to get up on his feet. Not quite yet, said Mom. This baby is special. He got up quickly on big strong legs. The umbilical cord broke separating the intimate connection to his

Momma. He fell right on his face and rolled over. Concerned, Mom looked over at him. Carefully rising to her feet, Momma gently reached out lovingly welcoming her new foal, licking him. She softly guided him as he maneuvered his way to his feet again. He fell onto his side. His next attempt, with his mother patiently waiting by the side, was successful as he teetered, weaving back and forth. Another whinny from Momma prompted his little mouth to begin suckling, which is so natural to newborn foals. Momma decided to lay down one more time to rest. The afterbirth, still hanging, has done its job.

This was a big bay colt with long legs. There was a beautiful star on his forehead. He had one white sock on the right front foot and another sock on his left hind foot with big expressive eyes, a wide forehead, tippy ears pointing inwards and a short exotic Arabian head. Nostrils flaring and breathing hard, he struggled to his feet. My pride was busting out all over. I was watching her give birth for the first time. We have struggled so long to get this pregnancy right. I whispered a prayer to my heavenly Father and thanked Him for this special event. A small voice, within, was telling me that this was meant to be. Have courage and be kind, such a familiar thought that I had come to cherish these past twenty years. My mind began to wander back to a special time in my life.

CHAPTER 2

The Horse Bug

It was a hot summer day. With our windows wide open, my mom and I drove down the road in our pickup, with a borrowed horse trailer attached, headed to the auction yard. We were going to rescue a horse. This was definitely different. Since Dad died, my Mom would accommodate me, but this time she thought I was nuts. The new farm only had enough room for some cows and chickens, but a horse; I'd wanted a horse for as long as I can remember. At sixteen years old, it had been my dream, but now it was going to become a reality.

My friend Steve called me and said, "Mathew, I found the perfect horse for you. You better get down here to the auction yard fast to rescue her, or else she will be sold to a meat buyer!"

We hastened our speed and pulled into the yard to meet Steve in just enough time as the number attached to the butt of this mare, number twenty-four, was read by the auctioneer. Luckily there weren't a lot of people there when we started the bidding. Across the way, we noticed a haggard old man, a killer buyer. This poor mare, from what we were told, was only there because her owners, a husband and wife, had died. They were local Arabian breeders. This mare was probably one of their best broodmares. She didn't look too bad. She was known to produce beautiful foals. My mom told me that she could give me the fifty dollars she had set aside. Steve was from a farm down the street. He had horses all his life. The bidding started on number twenty-four, Steve whispered and suggested twenty-five dollars. I confidently yelled out, "Twenty-five dollars!"

"Who bid thirty-five dollars, thirty-five dollars?" cried the auctioneer.

Without hesitation the guy across the way bid thirty-five dollars. It was the kill buyer. We looked at each other. We couldn't let this guy get that mare. We bid another ten dollars. Without a higher bid, the killer buyer was already up to fifty dollars. There was silence as Mom looked at me. The auctioneer's eyes moved from me to the kill buyer.

With determination, my Mom blurted out, "Seventy-five dollars!"

We couldn't believe it! The haggard old man stared at the floor and didn't answer.

The auctioneer yelled out, "Going once, going twice, sold for seventy-five dollars!"

My mom was as surprised as we were. We just sat there for a moment. Did that really just happen?

Steve accompanied us to the corral. There she was. We all looked at each other. The realization of what we'd done has just set in. Now what?

"This is a great horse, Mathew. When we get her back to your place, she's going to need some groceries and some tender loving care." Steve said, reassuring us. He continued pointing out all the great qualities of the mare. He took her lead and loaded her into the trailer.

This was really new. Since Dad died, it had been hard for Mom and me. The two years of fighting cancer finally took my dad. There were many visits to the hospital and to the doctor. Ironically, we spent more time together as a family during those two years because before Dad got sick, he was gone on many tours with the military. Not having Dad around had been tough. Primarily, the reason for moving from the big city to the little town of Alfalfa, east of Bend, Oregon, was to keep me out of trouble, Mom thought. It was a little hay farming community, surrounded by the Bureau of Land Management (BLM) acreage. There was a run-down, two-bedroom farmhouse that needed a little bit of fixing up, just big enough for Mom and me, with two or three outbuildings, a little barn with a couple of stalls. The fencing was all right, but it needed to be repaired. My bright idea to get a horse, especially this quick, came at a time when we were not prepared. With no experience, we hadn't even gotten any hay yet. For the new horse's safety, we put her in one of the stalls, temporarily, till we could fix the fences, and Steve loaned us some hay. Because Steve was going off to college, I was basically left on my own. Mom had very little knowledge of horses. I remember my father reading the book, *The Black Stallion*, to me when I was very young. Living in the middle of Los Angeles California, the closest horses were at Hollywood Park Racetrack, a few blocks from where we lived. My older sister took me, before dawn, to see the race horse's morning workouts. The feelings were almost indescribable as I soaked in the sights and smells surrounding me. There in front of me, appearing out of the mist was a strongly familiar sight: powerful horses as if I'd witnessed this before. I sold newspapers at the track, so I could watch the races. I really had the horse bug. There was no chance to have a horse back then. Now here we were with this beautiful and mysterious Arabian mare in our barn. It was getting late. Steve and I put some hay in the stall and gave her some water. I hung around for a while, making sure she was okay. The ordeal at her previous owner's ranch and at the feedlot auction yard took a big toll on her emotionally and physically, but she showed great courage. I wanted her to get along well. Mom suggested since it was so hot that I would stay in the barn and sleep on some hay next to her stall.

Mom said, "You know, I gave you that extra twenty-five dollars. I've got a lot of work to be done around here. You can work it off. Okay?"

I responded, "All right, Mom, I sure do love you. I think Dad would be proud of what we're doing right now, the work would be a good distraction. I always felt he was around in spirit."

CHAPTER 3

A Horse in the Barn

That first night in the barn with my new mare, hundreds of thoughts ran through my mind. I couldn't sleep. Mom had come to check on me with a hot cup of tea; it was soothing on those hot summer nights. "Just go to sleep. This will help," she said. I slept next to the stall.

Babe, as I called the new addition to our family, ate all her hay and drank all her water. I was so thankful that she did, knowing what she'd gone through. The smell of bacon and eggs and hot oatmeal was coming from the house. I got up, rubbed my eyes, ambled up to the house, and sat down. My mom gave me a big hug.

"How was your night Mathew? Did you sleep well?" Mom asked.

"As much as I could," I answered. "But really, I was worried about Babe."

"Babe?" asked Mom.

"Yep Mom, I decided to name her Babe."

"You think that fits her huh?" She asked.

"Yep." I paused. "I sure wish Steve wasn't going off to college because I have no idea what to do now. We got her home, and at least we have some hay. We need to go to the feed store today and get supplies and maybe some advice," I said.

After a good meal and some hot chocolate, we were off to do the chores.

"You really think we can leave her alone?" asked Mom.

"Mom, it's okay," I answered. "She'll be fine."

On the way back to return the trailer, we stopped at the feed store. Henry Miller, the store's proprietor, saw us coming up and said, "Word's gotten around that you got a really nice mare from that auction yesterday."

"Yes, we did," said Mom," but it's going to be interesting. You know anybody that can help us with this horse?"

"I do know someone," said Mr. Miller. "In fact, he lives right across the street from you. Want to check him out?"

"Anything can help right now. Thanks, Henry," Mom answered.

The community of Alfalfa was about ten square miles with an old Grange Hall, a place for families to meet for political and agricultural activities, and a general store with the only gas pump for twenty-five miles. There are a lot of hard-working people in this area, and because they grow a lot of hay, there are always trucks coming and going. Across the way from my house lived one of those truckers that Henry had mentioned. We would stop and wave while we were moving in. He had a big Freightliner semi truck parked in his driveway, a neat little farmhouse with a barn and fenced pasture. While this trucker was home, he would be outside tinkering with his truck. There was really no sign of life other than his presence. Is this the person Henry was talking about? Sure didn't look like it.

CHAPTER 4

The Trucker Across the Street

We had a lot of work to do that day if we wanted to put this horse outside somewhere. Our fences were in bad condition and not safe. The two stalls we had in the barn were knee deep in manure. With our severe lack of tools, we were not prepared. I ran into the house with an idea to pass by Mom.

"You know the man across the street looks like he might have some tools that we could borrow. I should go over there and ask him," I told her shrewdly.

"That's a good idea." She grinned.

I peeked out the door that direction and said, "I see him working on his truck. I'll be right back. Wish me luck."

The day was getting warmer as I ran across the street to approach this man who was busy underneath his truck. He was a middle-aged man with gray hair. He was wearing some old dirty overalls.

"Hello," I said. All I heard was hello coming back from underneath the truck.

"Who's there?" he asked.

"My name's Mathew. I live across the street."

Out from underneath the truck appeared a smiling face squinting at the sun as he looked at the sunrise in the distance. "What can I do for you, sonny?" He reached out his greasy hand for me to shake.

I didn't hesitate but clasped his hand eagerly.

"My name is Mike." As he withdrew his hand, realizing that he had just gotten grease all over me. "Sorry about that," he said as he wiped his hands on his overalls. "Your name is Mathew?" Mike asked.

"Yes sir, we just moved in across the street, and I wanted to come over and introduce myself," I said.

"Where did you move from, son?" asked Mike.

"We're really new to this area. We came up here from LA," I answered.

"This is really way out in the country. What made you come way out here?" he asked

"Well, my mom and I came up here after my Dad died. My Mom said that it would be good for me."

"Hey, how do you like it up here kid?" Mike asked.

"Well, I've never been anywhere so dark in my life. Down in LA, we had streetlights all over the place, and I've never seen so many animals before. There aren't any streetlights anywhere here either. You drive this big truck for a living?" I asked.

"Yep. I've been living in this truck for the last three years. I'm seldom home, but it's a living."

"You sure have a nice place here," I commented.

Mike longingly answered, "Yes, I really love it when I'm home."

"The reason why I am here, Mike, I wanted to ask you if you might have some tools that I could borrow. There are so many chores I have to do. You know, we just got this horse, and there's no place to put her," I told him.

"You just got a horse?" Mike asked.

"Yep. Just yesterday we went down to the auction and saved her from a killer buyer."

"Really!" You know what; I've been under this truck for so long. Maybe I should help you. I'd be glad to get you those tools. I'll help you take them over. Maybe you can show me this horse you have."

"Thanks so much," I said with gratitude.

"Just give me a second to clean off my hands. Here, come clean yours up, too. What do you think we'll need?"

"I have to clean out some stalls, and I have to fix the fence because it's down over there," I answered

"Let's see, shovels, pitchforks, and a wheelbarrow or two would probably work. I'll throw in some wire, a hammer, and nails with some staples. Once we get there, we can check things out," Mike suggested.

We went out to the barn and opened those big doors.

"Wow, look at all this stuff," I said.

"Yes, it'll be good to put this stuff to good use." Mike smiled.

"Look at all those saddles!" I said.

"We call that tack, and it has been gathering dust for the last three years."

With all the necessary items gathered together in two wheelbarrows, I was thankful that Mike was there to help me out. A nicker rang out from the barn as we opened the door. There were two ears pointing at attention with big eyes looking our way.

"Is this the horse you're talking about?" Mike asked.

"Yes, it is, what do you think?" I responded as we approached the door of the stall.

"Is it okay if I go in with her?" Mike asked.

"Sure, this is the first horse I've ever had, and I sure need help. I know that she's really pretty, but I need another opinion. You know anything about horses?"

"Yeah, a little bit," Mike answered as he went up to the door to let the horse see him.

Curiously, Babe moved closer and smelled Mike's arm.

"Good girl," praised Mike.

I was really glad that Babe was interested. It seemed like Mike was able to help her feel at ease. It looked like Mike was getting her permission to enter the stall. I stood there watching curiously as Mike opened the door gently and proceeded inside. Standing inside quietly, Mike allowed Babe to approach him. Reaching out, he touched her softly, "It looks like she's in pretty good shape. Do you know how old she is?"

"No, I don't," I said.

"Well let me see." Mike gently reached up and opened her mouth. He just looked in there and said, "Well, looks like she's about seven or eight years old."

"How do you know that? You can tell by looking in her mouth?" I asked.

"Yes, I'm just looking at her teeth," Mike answered.

"Wow, you can really do that?"

"You're just full of questions, aren't you."

"Well, this is new to me, but, do you like her?" I asked.

"I do." Mike smiled. "She's a good size. What do you want to do with her?"

"When I was young, I saw a bunch of horses at a racetrack, and since then I wanted a horse so bad. I really want to ride her," I replied.

"Do you know if she's ride-able?" Mike asked.

"I really don't know. This horse is all I've got. I don't even know her history." I said.

"Well you know, from what I can tell, this is an Arabian. Not only is she purebred but she is well bred. Is there any way that you can get her history for me?" Mike asked.

"Wow, they said she came from an Arabian breeder! Maybe I can go and find out some more information about her," I said excitedly.

"That would really be a great idea," Mike told me.

"There's a lot of work ahead of us. Let's get started," Mike said as he looked at the stall next door. "Let's clean that stall first, then we can move ... what's her name?"

I answered, "I call her Babe."

Mike continued, "We can move Babe to the next stall when we're finished. I can almost guarantee you that she has a real name. We can find out that from the breeder, I hope."

Boy, that stall was deep. It took about two hours with both of us working hard in the heat with sweat rolling down our brows and our T-shirts all wet. Mom came out and offered us some lemonade.

"Oh, hi Mom. I want to introduce you to Mike."

As Mike reached out with his dirty hand, he said, "Pleased to meet you, Ma'am.

"My name is Marcia," she said as she gingerly shook his hand. "I wanted to thank you for helping my son. Mathew is so excited about this horse. He didn't even sleep last night."

"You're welcome Ma'am, I mean Marcia, if you don't mind?"

"Sure, can I call you Mike?"

"No problem. With us hot and sweaty, I appreciate your thinking about us Marcia."

"It looks like you're getting along there pretty well," Marcia said as she noticed that it was almost noon. "May I invite you for some lunch?"

"Well, that's very kind of you Ma'am, but we just have one more stall to do here., We'll be in when it's finished," he said. Mike turned to me. "What do you think Mathew, it looks like you can handle those tools very well. Have you ever done this before?"

I looked at Mike and said, "I really never have. I'm just following what you do."

Mike continued, "Now that we have this stall done get that bale of straw, and we'll put it in here. Hey, do you have a halter?"

I got the halter off the wall and handed it to Mike. He quietly entered the stall and put the halter on Babe. We went ahead and moved her over to the next stall, which was freshly bedded. Mike then took the halter off, and we moved the water and some fresh hay over. She proceeded to roll in the new bedding, almost like she was thanking us for the trouble that we had gone to. We went ahead and cleaned the other stall and got it prepared. By that time, we were both pretty hungry.

Mom had lunch ready in the house. Before we got into the house, Mom called out, "You guys better cleanup. You stink to high heavens."

"Yes Mom," I answered. " Follow me, I'll show you to the bathroom, Mike."

Marcia had the table nicely set with some ice-cold lemonade. She had made grilled cheese along with some peanut butter and jelly sandwiches. I devoured four sandwiches to feed my growing body. Mom was glad to provide us everything we needed to refuel us, so we could get back to work. Living in the city was definitely a contrast compared to all this hard work. "I really appreciate you helping my son, Mike." Mom said with gratitude.

"You're welcome, Marcia. I thought it would be important to help Mathew get this mare situated so she can be safe. We just have to get some fencing outside taken care of. I have time today to help him before going to work tonight, on another run."

"Sure appreciate it," I said thankfully.

There was already a corral that needed repair, with a few boards down. We repaired the boards and rehung the gate. That corral was right outside, adjoining, both the stalls. We opened the door, and Babe curiously ventured out to her new surroundings.

As Mike watched Babe, he said, "This is one step closer to turning her out into the big pasture. It looks like she's eating all her feed, and she's drinking her water. When I get back from my run, I'll come over and help you fix the wire fencing in the pasture." Mike continued, "While I'm gone, could you check at the auction yard regarding any information you can gather on her background and breeding? Here, I'll write it down for you. She is bay, around seven or eight years old with a star and stripe on her face, a sock on her right hind leg and a coronet on her left front."

"I sure will. Thank you, Mike." I answered.

"Let's leave these wheelbarrows and tools here, they are just gathering dust at my place," said Mike.

I went ahead and accompanied Mike across the street back to his barn. Mike invited me into his tack room. As we sat down Mike's demeanor became rather serious. He had something important to share with me.

Mike began, "I have an assignment for you, Mathew. When you're there with your horse, go into her stall and her corral and just sit there. I want you to just sit there quietly and let her get used to you. Just let her come up to you when she's ready, don't reach out to her. Let her touch you first. I want you to write down anything that you see and note your observations. When I see you next, I'll ask you what those things were, okay?"

"Sure I will," I answered. "How long do you think you'll be gone?"

"Oh, usually, about two days."

"All right, be safe out there. Bye," I said as I ran across the street and headed over next to Babe's stall and just stood there at the door, looking in on her. It'd been a long day with a lot of hard work, and the realization of what she now meant to me. Wishing I could wrap my arms around her, I gave my new mare a flake of hay and some water. I headed into the house where my mother met me at the door. I hugged her like I'd never had before. Mom, knowing my heart, sweetly hugged me back. Dinner was ready. I ate a hearty meal and headed right up to bed. I could hardly wait to get back to work tomorrow with the assignment that Mike had given me. No sooner had I hit the pillow, I fell fast asleep.

CHAPTER 5

My Majestic Princess

While living in the big city, it seemed like it was always daytime. In the country before the sun comes up, we have the birds singing, the chickens across the way crowing and the rays of the sun pouring through the window to welcome the new day. I could smell bacon cooking, and the rich aroma of coffee from downstairs. Mom called up to me and said that breakfast was ready. I could hear Mom's classical music playing as I threw on my clothes and ran down to the kitchen. While we sat talking about the day's chores, I asked Mom if there was any way that we could go into town to the auction yard to get some more information on Babe. She said that was a great suggestion and we'd do that as soon as possible. But first, I needed to go out and take care of my mare.

Once my morning chores were completed, we were on our way to town. The feed store was the first stop. Henry, the feed store owner, was happy to help us with what we needed. He suggested we get some hay and grain. We found out that there was much more than just feeding a horse hay and grain. Mr. Miller said that we needed to put her on an anti-parasite program. That would involve the local veterinarian, Dr. Jim Edmonds, DVM, who can help us with her complete health. I was glad we had such friendly people to help us out. Mr. Miller asked us if we had contacted our neighbor across the street, Mr. Chapman. We had just found out that was Mike's last name, Mike Chapman. We shared with Mr. Miller that Mr. Chapman was helping us with my new horse and surprised us with all his knowledge. The store owner assured us that we could trust Mr. Chapman completely. I thanked him for everything, and we proceeded to the auction yard.

The auction yard owner was helpful in answering our questions. The previous owners of Babe were not available since they had passed away, but he gave us information, including a phone number, about their next of kin. We thanked the owner and headed down to the phone booth. The phone rang, and we got an answer.

"Hello," I said, "my name is Mathew, and I bought a horse that used to belong to the Maxwell family. Is that your mother and father's name?"

The voice on the other end of the phone answered, "Yes."

I asked if they had any information on the horses that they used to own. The man on the other end of the line was happy to help us. It was the son who had worked on getting all the records together after his parent's deaths.

He asked, "what else do you need to know."

I told him that we had bought a mare, at the auction yard in Bend, Oregon, and I read him the paper that Mike had given me. "Okay," I said. "She is bay, around seven or eight years old with a star and stripe on her face, a sock on her right hind leg and a coronet on her left front." I asked them if there was anything else I might need to give them to help identify her? The reply was that we were really in luck because they had held that horse back for a long time before sending her to auction and that she was the best horse his parents had. He explained that they went as long as they could, trying to get her a safe home, but because of circumstances beyond their control, they were forced to take her to the auction. The son asked if she was doing okay. I told him that we were able to get her out of that auction yard before the kill buyer got hold of her. I explained that she was doing great at our home now. I told him that we named her Babe. After a pause, he informed me that he did have the information on this horse. As he looked further, he found that she was registered with the Arabian Horse Association and he had all her papers. He said that he knew that his parents would have liked her to be registered with the new owners, and he'd be glad to give them to me.

"By the way," I said, "I want to put my Mom on the phone because she is just so thankful."

Mom took the receiver and said, "Sir, thank you so much for doing this for us. My son and I are going to take good care of her."

"You're very welcome Ma'am, let me get your address and number, and I'll be glad to send all this paperwork to you. I'm over in the valley. It should be to you in a couple days."

It was exciting to get this information, we were anxious to know just what we had. The breeder's son said that the Arabian mare from their breeding program was very special. Were we really that fortunate? We could hardly wait to find out what we had. Over the weekend, I was busy mending fences, taking care of Babe, and preparing to put her out in a bigger pasture enclosure. Babe had settled in quite nicely. The time I spent sitting in her paddock just watching her was paying off. Many times, she would come up to me and sniff me. As Mike told me, I just sat there and made observations. I wrote down everything, so I could report to Mike when he came back.

With much anticipation, I was waiting at the mailbox on Monday. There was a big manila envelope addressed to me from the relatives that we spoke to over in the valley. I couldn't wait to open it, but I knew that my mom wanted to be there. So I took it right into the house, and we opened it together. Eagerly, we read the contents. "Dear Mathew and Marcia. We're so thankful that you were able to get my parents' precious mare and give her a loving home. You said that you named her Babe, her real name is My Majestic Princess, and she is eight years old. Enclosed are her registration papers with my signature, transferring ownership. Also, a copy of all her medical treatment and her breeding record is enclosed. She has had two foals. I wish you a lot of success in the future. Take good care of her. My parents are looking down smiling, knowing that she is in good hands. Yours truly, Pat and Joanna."

I was outside one morning when I heard a big truck rumbling down the road. Mike was home, and I was so excited to tell him what I'd found out. Before he could open the door, I was over there beckoning him to roll down the window with the dust billowing all over. He waited until it settled before he opened the door to greet me.

"Howdy Mathew. How are you?"

"I'm fine, thank you, Mike. How are you?"

"I'm tired, went all the way up into Canada this time to deliver that load of hay. I got caught up at the border with customs. It took me about twelve hours just to clear that load because they said that they had some kind of mold on it, but I'm glad I'm back home. By the way, how is your mare doing?"

I quickly answered, "Oh, she's doing fantastic. I've been spending a lot of time in her stall. I have so many things to tell you. What I've found out about her, things that I see when I sit there next to her and, oh my goodness, we got some information on the past owners."

"Settle down for a second. Let me get this truck turned around and go get cleaned up, and then I'll come on over."

"Oh, okay, thanks. We'll be waiting for you."

Mike appeared at the door of the barn, and he commented on how clean the barn was.

"You've been doing a lot of work; put my tools to good use," praised Mike.

I quickly nodded in appreciation but anxiously motioned him over to Babe's stall, then I said, "I've been doing what you told me to do. I spend hours out there sitting in the paddock with her. I wrote down a lot of things that I observed. I haven't done anything with her yet. I am so anxious to do something. You think you can teach me how to put a halter on her?"

"Well, sure." Mike smiled. "She's looking good, gaining a little bit of weight." Just then she put her head over the door to greet us.

"Now, that's a good sign. She's settling in nicely."

My Mom appeared in the door of the barn, and in her hand was the manila envelope. We gathered together where the light was brighter and opened the envelope. Mike was anxious to look at her pedigree. Just one look and Mike froze. He became silent as he looked a little bit closer. To make sure that he saw it correctly, he put on his glasses.

"Could you excuse me for a moment," Mike said. He went outside and went around the corner.

I asked Mom, "What was that all about?"

In a little bit, he reappeared and excused himself for being so emotional. "It's a long story, and please excuse me. It's a great pedigree, fantastic as a matter of fact." Mike became strangely silent and changed the subject. "My Majestic Princess. What a beautiful name. What are you going to do now Mathew? Are you going to nickname her Babe?"

I thoughtfully answered, "I'll think about that. Give me some time to get to know her a little bit better."

"Keep up the good work. Babe looks good and healthy. Excuse me folks, I'm tired, and I'm going to go back home and get some sleep. I've been on the road for three days straight and I'll … I'll catch you guys later."

"Thank you, Mike," said Marcia.

"I hope you get some good rest. Will you be coming over tomorrow?" I interjected expectantly.

"Sure, I'll see you tomorrow. Thank you, Ma'am, I mean Marcia. I'm sure you're very proud of your son. Good night."

And with that Mike excused himself and went across the street.

Very concerned I asked, "Mom, what do you think that was all about? Suddenly, he got really weird. What happened? Do you think he didn't like her or something?"

"I don't know, son, but just let him get some rest. He's been driving for a long time. He'll be all right. I know it was rough when we were driving up from LA. He drives all the time."

"Okay, I understand. In the meantime, I'll just keep on taking good care of our 'little Miya', wow, what do you think, Mom? You think Miya would be a good name?"

"Well, maybe you want to think on that one. Get your chores done. Then come on in. We have an early meeting tonight at the Grange Hall." With that, I hurriedly fed, watered, and gave my special girl her first big hug.

CHAPTER 6

The New Foal

Suddenly hearing a familiar noise from the gray mare brought my mind back to the present. Seeing the big bay colt, still wobbly, trying to get his balance, as Mom, now back up on her feet, squealed as she encouraged the baby to nurse. Her afterbirth had just cleared. I gathered it up and set it aside. You could see her sides were busily contracting. That didn't bother her. She was nuzzling the baby, nickering softly, pushing her newborn toward the leaky teats that were pouring milk from underneath her with the precious colostrum awaiting consumption by this newborn. Patiently, she guided the little colt to start nursing. Missing the mark, sliding under Mom, she winced and squealed as the baby went bouncing off the wall. Gathering himself back up he persistently searched, as he suckled, for that elusive faucet. His little muzzle brushed the swollen teats and milk shot out, covering his little face. He must have thought it tasted pretty good because his tongue suckled more, finding that little teat, latching onto it, getting a big shot of colostrum. Satisfied, the bay colt crashed back down onto the soft straw and drifted off to sleep. While he was sleeping, I was able to paint the umbilical cord with iodine to protect him against infection and gave him an enema to encourage his first bowel movement. He barely even moved. The dream of getting a foal from this beautiful mare was finally fulfilled. I was so proud. All involved had worked for so long. But here he was, surpassing all our expectations. Double checking all the necessary precautions for the newborn and the mare, I decided it was okay for me to go to bed, leaving them alone to get acquainted. Before going to sleep, my mind drifted back in time to when Mom and I were preparing to leave for Grange Hall.

CHAPTER 7

The Grange Hall

Mom called me to come back into the house, reminding me about the early dinner at the Grange Hall. I asked my Mom again what she thought about what happened with Mike today. She said that she didn't know what to think and that it was really odd. It was almost like he was sad. "I'll tell you what, Mathew, I'm going to check around to see if I can find out something more about Mike. I will be getting involved at the Grange. They have a meeting there tonight after dinner. Maybe I can ask some of the people in the community if they know much about Mike."

I thought Mom had a great idea and then I said, "Maybe there will be some young ladies down there I can meet. What do you think?"

Chuckling, Mom responded, "You're growing up too fast. The dinner and meeting starts at seven."

It was dark over at Mike's house as we drove out of the driveway. It looked like he had retired early. Five miles down the road was a large building that served as the Grange Hall. This area was settled eighty years ago. At that time there was a rather large lake close by. It was rather shallow, fed by the snow of the surrounding mountains. The climate was much wetter then. Looking in the distance, you can see a vast dry lake bed that replaced the big lake. Now it was a fertile place to raise many different hay crops because of the volcanic soils. The canal system for irrigation put in place about sixty years ago, in the Deschutes

River Valley of Central Oregon, along with fertilization, made the desert bloom. The elevation of 3,500 feet was a perfect climate, free from the Pacific storms that thrashed the Willamette Valley across the Cascade Range to the west. The high desert of Central Oregon was the perfect climate for hay production.

The parking lot was full. People had their potluck dinners in their arms as they made their way into the hall. We were met at the door by a nice gentleman. He was the pastor of the little assembly that met at the Grange Hall every Sunday. He introduced himself to us and others as they came in.

Poking me, Mom said, "Come on in Mathew. Let's sit."

I was a little distracted. There were a couple young ladies that drew my attention. Mom and I grabbed a seat on the benches where the picnic tables were all set up inside. There were paper plates with a nice setting in front of us of salads and potatoes. Off to the side, people were lining up to get the main course of hamburgers and hotdogs. For the specialty, there was rib eye steak cooked outside. The aroma was wonderful. From time to time my attention was seriously distracted. Right in front of me was a girl that caught my attention. Her name was Shirley. She had on cowboy boots. I asked her if I could sit next to her. Congenially, she agreed. As I slid closer to her, she looked at her girlfriend and giggled. In our conversation, about horses, her interest piqued, then she told me about the 4-H club that she was involved in and invited me to join.

Mom was busy making acquaintances. She was very amazed at how friendly everybody was compared to how things were in the big city. Soon the conversation turned to her question about our neighbor, Mike. Mr. Jeffers said that he knew Mike was a good trucker. He had been driving for about three years now. Bob Jeffers was overheard by an older gentleman, Tom Hoffman, who excused himself and said that he was quite sure that Mike used to live over in the valley. He mentioned that Mike's last name was Chapman. He said that he had been over in

Alfalfa for a short time, but he lived in the valley for about twenty years in Portland. I heard that he was involved with horses, in fact, heavily involved with horses. "Now wait a minute," my Mom said. "Are you sure that's the Mike Chapman who lives down there off Walker Road?"

"Yes, I'm quite sure about it," answered Mr. Hoffman. "He's the truck driver, right?"

"Yes, drives a big black Freightliner."

"Yes, that's right, that's who I'm talking about," Mom exclaimed. "Well, if he was involved in horses a lot, what's he doing over here?" she asked. "We don't see any evidence of life over there. No horses, no dogs. He's just in his truck all the time." Mom wondered.

As Mom questioned a few more members of the Grange the common answer seemed to be, "I don't know the whole story." It was very difficult for her to get any more information about Mike. That really sparked her interest. Now she was very curious. Mom thanked Tom. After a delicious meal with many new friends and a wonderful conversation, I was busily talking horses with Shirley. I told Mom that I was excited because Shirley told me about a 4-H club that I could join, all about horses.

"That's great," Mom said, "You have a lot to look forward to with new friends here." Satisfied with our introduction to the community, we headed home.

CHAPTER 8

Who Is Mike Chapman?

The next day as I woke up, I noticed that the big Freightliner across the street was gone. I was disappointed because Mike had said that he'd come over today. Mike must have had to make another run. Miya was waiting for me at her stall door. Mike said to take it slow, but I had advanced to putting the halter on Miya. It was hard sometimes to see which way it went on, however. I invited my friend Shirley to come out, and she showed me the right way to do it. It was great to have someone my age who knew how to care for horses. She showed me how to lead Miya, groom her, and clean out her feet. She asked me if I would like to come to the next 4-H meeting at the Grange Hall on Thursday. I was excited and said that would be great. She said it would give me a chance to meet some of the other girls and boys in the community. She said that maybe I could bring my horse to the next horse play day at the fairgrounds. It would be on Saturday. I didn't have a horse trailer, so I asked Shirley if she might have room for Miya in her trailer. Shirley's parents are leaders in the 4-H club. I could hardly wait to tell Mike about this. I truly hoped he would be home soon because it would be nice if he came along. I was thinking that, maybe, he would like to be a leader.

Mom was busy on the phone. Armed with Mike's last name, she tracked down where Mike had lived for so long over in the Willamette

Valley. With a lot of effort, one great connection potentially provided Mike's parent's phone number. She dialed excitedly. "Maybe we can get some questions answered here," she thought. "Hello, is this Mrs. Chapman? My name is Marcia Peters. I'm calling from over in Central Oregon."

"Yes, this is Mrs. Chapman. Hello Marcia, what can I do for you?"

"We recently met a Mike Chapman who lives across the street from us in Alfalfa, near Bend. Is this your relation?" Mom asked.

"Yes, he's been living over there for about three years now. I know; indeed, he lives over in Alfalfa," answered Mrs. Chapman.

"We just moved to the area, and he was very kind to share some information about caring for a horse that we had recently purchased. I wanted to thank him, but he is off driving his truck now. Could you tell me something about, well, excuse me, I was just a little bit concerned because of an incident that happened at our place when we were sharing information about our new horse with him. When he saw the pedigree of our new horse, he suddenly got very quiet and very emotional. I'm a little bit worried about him because he just changed the subject, excused himself, and went home. I know he was rather tired, but he said that he would come over the next day. We noticed his truck was gone the next day. I don't want to pry, but he's all by himself over there with no family that we could see. He has been so kind to my son, and we have come to enjoy his company. Could you tell us something that would help us understand his reaction?"

"Thank you, Ms. Peters, for your concern," said Mrs. Chapman. Then she continued. "Mike really isn't a truck driver at heart. He's been living in his truck most of the time for the last three years. I really haven't heard from him a lot." Mike's mom asked, "Is he okay?"

"He was very happy when he was with our horse, Mrs. Chapman, that's why we were so concerned when he just excused himself."

"Mrs. Peters, did you say that he was looking at a pedigree of a horse when he got all emotional?"

"Yes, that's what happened," Mom explained.

"Mrs. Peters, I'll share this with you. It just kills Mike to be in his truck all the time. He is a horseman from way back; ever since he could walk. He's been chasing horses all over the country and the world for most of his life. Thirteen years ago, his business failed and all that kept his family alive were his horses. He was forced to start driving a truck to make a living. His saving grace was a special stallion that he imported from Germany. He worked hard to keep his horse ranch running while he stood his stallion on his ranch. He loved that stallion dearly. He was his soul mate. It was hard to balance the work at the ranch, driving, and breeding many mares while taking care of his family. Three years ago, his precious stallion died. The stress on his wife because of finances, his absence while driving, and the death of their beloved family stallion was too much. That's when his wife divorced him, taking his son. They owned thirty or more mares at the time, which resulted in the disbursement of all those priceless horses that he had bred over the years. It was very difficult for Mike; he sunk into a deep depression as he drove his truck. Not being able to have his precious horses by his side, I'm glad to see that at least he came over to see your horse because I think he believed he would never have a horse again. I appreciate your sharing this with me Mrs. Peters."

With great empathy, Mom said, "It must be hard for you Mrs. Chapman to see this happening to him. My son has become good friends with Mike, and he really looks up to him. My son probably reminds Mike of his own son who lives with his mother. Does he get to see him very often Mrs. Chapman?"

"Well, I don't know how long it's been since he has seen him. His family is moving around the country, and I guess one of the reasons why he is driving his truck for work is so he could be close to him and maybe visit with him now and again," Mrs. Chapman explained.

"Thank you for sharing this, ma'am. It helps me to understand what happened in the barn the other day. Would it be okay if I save your number and keep you informed?" Mom said.

"My son is really a good man Mrs. Peters. There is no reason to worry about him associating with your son."

"I really appreciate that Mrs. Chapman. I'll keep you posted. Thank you again. Goodbye."

CHAPTER 9

Mike's Depression

Slowly climbing the big grade the next morning up to the Mount Hood Summit, Mike grabbed another gear, allowing his thirty tons of precious hay to inch closer to his destination near Seattle. He was up early that morning putting together his combination of truck, forty-foot trailer, and twenty-foot dolly trailer. The dairy cattle would get four deliveries a week of these twenty-two bales of alfalfa, and each bale weighed about 1,400 pounds. It was hard work strapping down the hay and possibly having to put a tarp over it to keep it dry. Living in the great Northwest, there was a saying that liquid sunshine is the forecast for the day. He usually didn't take that trip, but what occurred that night across the street at the barn had bothered him. The depression that had been eating at him was like a thick fog that would not leave him. It was hard, not to go over there that morning. He just wasn't ready. Just imagining someone doing something normal in their lives was very difficult for Mike. That's what his depression did. It was painful. Somehow, being in the truck took away that fog and gave him something to do. For three years that's how his life had been.

Long stretches of time driving gave Mike the opportunity for deep thoughts that he would share with me. With God as his only companion, he shared his feelings, emotions, heartaches, dreams, and desires with Him. "I'm sorry, God, I just don't have courage anymore, but I sure loved seeing that horse last night. After looking at that pedigree and seeing that it was a mare that had come from my breeding program, I just broke down. The Peters' must have thought I was inconsiderate, excusing myself. I feel so bad about that, dear God."

He'd always been attracted to horses, and then he saw that first Arabian horse that he fell in love with. He remembered his Mom telling him that he couldn't go down to Catalina Island by himself at sixteen years old and work on an Arabian horse ranch. But he did anyway. It was hard for his mom to control him. He was so hardheaded. The image in his head of that magnificent horse was too deep in his spirit. He just couldn't shake it. He remembered praying at night thanking God for creating the horse and allowing him to be with them. Nothing would stop him. He really drove his mother nuts, building a little paddock in his backyard, spending all the money he had and all the time he had after school just being with his horses. There were motorcycles, music, band, singing, sports, and so many distractions. He was so ADD.

He remembered that night after the senior all-night party after graduation. He had to be over in Middletown California on an Arabian horse ranch at eight o'clock in the morning and literally got no sleep that night. But he was there. What was the use of being in one place seeing only a few horses when he could go out and see the world, see as many horse ranches as possible and as many Arabian horses as possible. It was a real slow start trying to get his horse transport business started. He wished there had been more people to help him. His poor old truck and trailer weren't holding up. He was getting as many hauls as possible. He remembered that time when he was coming home from San Francisco after delivering a horse when he was running out of gas and rolled literally into the gas station out of gas. That was not very much fun. He was thankful that Robert Thompson gave him that job in his horse transport company. He told him, "Don't waste all that money getting your business going when you can just work for me." That was a good idea because that summer he drove thousands of miles exhausted, but he was just in heaven.

He had never seen so many horses in his life and met so many people that share the same passion that he did. When he got so tired he thought maybe a little change would be good for him. Well, what an abrupt change he made going up there to the Seattle area to work for five different horse ranches. He sure didn't make much money doing that plus working at McDonald's to try to make enough money to at least eat. That didn't last long! Somehow, he finagled a job down in Shreveport, Louisiana, working for a rich guy who wanted to start an Arabian horse ranch and spend about $3 million doing it. He was his man.

"Come on down, and we'll do it together," he'd said.

Well, he sure did go down there. He went for about six months. He did all the odd jobs but never laid a hand on a horse while the man tried to decide if he wanted to follow through with his idea. Then he brought him into his office and told him, "Well son, I decided to go into Appaloosas instead. My lawyer raises Appaloosas, so, you want to work for me now?"

He couldn't believe that, sitting there just literally in disbelief. He had wasted all that time. "Of course I don't want to work for an Appaloosa rancher," he said. "I came down here to work with Arabian horses. Gads no, I'm going back now to a truck that's broken down, after giving away everything I had, selling all my horses, and giving my dog Jake away just to come down here!"

He was so glad that those people back home took him in and let him sleep on the couch while he got his life back together. Well, one good thing was that he learned a lot. He learned how to put everything he knew into building a horse ranch. Learned a lot about bloodlines, and especially, he had learned to trust his intuition about who he shouldn't work for.

With no wheels, hitchhiking thirty miles every day built his character. Nothing was going to keep him away from Arabian horses. What an opportunity it was to go down there, to the McKenzie River Valley, and work for that Arabian horse ranch. For two years he took care of forty horses by himself: working, building, conditioning, training, and breeding. He especially gained a lot of knowledge there. He saw to it that twenty out of twenty mares got pregnant. Next year, he had sixty Arabians to take care of. He thought he was in heaven. Something that really drove him was this thing in his head: that Arabian horses were a part of him, that he had been with them forever. He thanked God for creating them.

Frustrated, Mike would wish he could get out of that truck and be back with his precious kindred spirits. But the reality was that he had to make a living, and this is all he had at the time.

CHAPTER 10

You Know Me Too Well

"Mom, can I go with Shirley on Thursday to the Grange Hall for the 4-H meeting?" I enthusiastically asked as I bounced down the front porch stairs.

"Sure. That's going to be a great opportunity for you. How are you doing with Miya?" Mom asked as she continued to hang the laundry in the warm summer sun.

"Oh Mom, I've been down to the barn brushing Miya. She's starting to put on some weight. I'm learning so much about horses from Shirley. She's a great horse hand. Besides, she's pretty." I smiled as I rolled in the green grass in front of Mom. "I think I've got a crush on her."

"That doesn't surprise me, Mathew, you handsome kid. All the women are going to be swooning over you."

Blushing, I said, "Oh Mom, there's more than just girls in that club," I stood up, red-faced. Lowering my voice, I said, "Maybe a lot of guys have horses too."

"Well, you can't hide it. You're growing up. Remember what I taught you," Mom mused. "Mathew, tell me what time the meeting is, so I can get you there."

"Oh, don't worry, Mom. Shirley's coming to pick me up on Thursday. On Saturday we take the horses to the fairgrounds for a play day. We get together and play games with the horses and learn how to ride properly, have lessons and get prepared for horse shows. There's a big trail ride a month from now, too. You think I can get Miya ready for that?"

"Remember, you've only ridden rental horses with your sister. However, I'm sure you'll get a lot of instruction this Saturday, and I truly hope you're not rushing into riding Miya." Mom cautioned. Hesitating, grabbing my shirt sleeve, Mom asked, "Wait a minute, you didn't do what I think you did, did you?"

I looked straight at Mom and said as we both laughed, "Well, you know me, Mom. I got the nerve to climb on her back yesterday while she was in the stall and it surprised me that she didn't do a thing. She seemed to trust me as she looked around at me. She's so sweet after everything she's gone through. Don't worry, Mom—I feel confident. I'm going to be the best owner she's ever had."

CHAPTER 11

A Little Horse Therapy

Mike's routine trip to that dairy in Washington became more bearable. Mike had exclaimed to me, "It was usually a lonely trip back to Alfalfa, but I was really looking forward to getting back home. I wanted to apologize to your family." Besides, it was nice for him being up on Mount Hood during the summer. The temperatures are at least twenty degrees cooler than the valley. Going down the other side, looking out at the Central Oregon High Desert is a sight to behold. "This is God's country" he would say. The fresh air of the Cascade Mountains revived him this time. He could hardly wait to get home and get cleaned up. Being exposed to a horse again after so long kind of shook him. But, just the memory of the sights and smells in that barn, combined with the beautiful morning, was starting to put a little sunshine in his life. "I wonder how Mathew is doing with his new charge?" He was concerned for once, it felt good, "My Majestic Princess, was, by the way, out of my old mare, Countess Majestic, which was one of the first mares that I bred."

Rolling into the driveway, Mike turned around and parked the truck next to his house, followed by a big cloud of dust. Central Oregon was pretty dry that time of year.

The next morning as the sun rose, poking its warm rays through the window, Mike woke up. "It's nice to be in my own bed at home", he thought. "I feel a little bit better this morning. It was good to get all that out of my mind that last trip". The thought of going across the street to see that beautiful mare gave Mike a little pep in his step. Mom and I were already up. I was out feeding my mare and doing the morning chores while Mom prepared breakfast.

CHAPTER 12

Mike's Passion Rekindled

"Hi Miya. How are you? Eating all your food and drinking your water? Good girl. I see that Mike is home. When I get done here, I'm gonna run over there and see if I can get some tools for the fencing so you can get out into the big pasture," I told her. The aroma of Mom's cooking filled the barn. I headed back to the kitchen and asked her, "Mom, did you notice that Mike is home? I'm going over there after breakfast to see him."

"Yes, I saw the lights from his truck late last night, I'm anxious to see how he's doing, as well," Mom answered. "Maybe he'll come over and see Miya; you have so much to show him since he's been gone."

I quickly ate my breakfast, and before Mom could say goodbye, I was out the door, running across the street to Mike's. I knocked on his door anxiously, calling, "Hello Mike, hello."

Mike came to the door cheerfully greeting me.

I blurted out, "I sure missed you. Did you have to drive again?"

Mike replied with remorse, "Yes, I'm sorry I didn't come over the other day. I wanted to apologize to you for not keeping my promise."

"Oh, that's okay. How soon can you come over? I want to show you everything that I've done to fix up the barn. The stall and the fencing are great. And can I borrow some more tools to finish the fencing? My poor Miya is cooped up in that little tiny paddock, and I would love to get her out in the big pasture."

Noting my excitement, Mike smiled and said, "Sure, let's go get the tools. Before we do that, I want to show you something special out in my barn."

Together, we walked out to the barn and opened those big doors. On the left was a tack room full of dusty saddles and bridles, brushes and horsey things. Astonished, I looked at Mike.

"Do you have a saddle?" Mike asked.

Bewildered I said, "No, I don't have anything. Mom and I got some brushes, but that's all."

Mike motioned toward me, "Come over here for a second. Let's measure your leg, okay that should be just about perfect." Mike pulled out a western saddle and put it on a saddle rack with a saddle pad and a bridle. "You know all this tack isn't getting used, so it might as well get used by you especially since you're sort of related, with a daughter of someone from my family over there." Mike laughed.

I looked at Mike awkwardly, but I thought, daughter? Letting that go, I said, "Oh Mike, thank you so much."

Mike loaded the saddle and tack into a wheelbarrow. We both headed across the street with wheelbarrow loaded with tack and tools. Now we were ready to fix the fence in the pasture. By this time, Miya was out in her paddock. Hearing the rattle of the wheelbarrow coming across the street, Mom poked her head out the back door. Mike noticed Mom on the porch and said, "Oh, hello Mrs. Peters, how are you today?"

"I'm fine, but how are you?" Mom answered.

"I'm very well thank you. In fact, I'm much better." Mike replied.

"We're really glad to see you, Mike. Mathew has so much to tell you. Give me a second, and I'll come out to the barn and join you. I've got to turn something off on the stove. Oh, and please call me Marcia."

Mike said, "No problem, ma'am … I mean Marcia."

Mike and I laughed as both of us men headed out to the barn. Hearing that noisy wheelbarrow, Miya came into the barn peeking over the stall door wondering what all that racket was.

"Aren't you looking lovely," Mike said to Miya. "Mathew, you sure are a lucky young man."

Just then Marcia joined the crew as they were busily unloading the wheelbarrow.

Mike stopped what he was doing and turned to my mom and said, "It's nice that you are here. I wanted to apologize to both of you for leaving abruptly the other night. I hope you will excuse me, but taking that last unscheduled trip has really helped me. It's been really difficult for me lately. This beautiful Arabian mare here … Well you know, I have to tell you something that will really surprise you both. When I looked at the registration papers for your mare, it was déjà vu. I bred this mare's mother."

Mom and I blurted simultaneously, "Really? You bred little Miya's mom?"

"Miya. That's what we call her," I added.

Mike, with emotion, stood next to my little Miya, looked into her soft eyes, and said, "Yep, long time ago, Countess Majestic, she was one of my first broodmares. I knew that I recognized the quality of your mare. She is so much like her mother. I'm an Arabian horse breeder, Mathew. It's a long story. You may not think so, seeing me driving my truck all the time, but these horses are deep within my soul. I want to ask you both. Do you believe in God? Because I believe strongly that we were all created together by God. You, me, and our horses. We were meant to come down to earth to be together, ultimately. I don't know about you, but ever since I was a little boy, I would pray to God and thank him for my family. Since I could walk, I had this passion for horses. I would ask God for that perfect horse to come into my life. I feel like I was really blessed."

"You know, when Dad was alive, we as a family, including my sister, used to go to church."

"You have a sister?"

"Yes. She's much older than me, and she left to go to college about six years ago. Marion would always tell me, 'oh, horse this and horse that'. I kinda caught the horse bug. L.A. has lots of concrete; whereas here, it's just big, open spaces. I couldn't really have a horse down there, only rental horses. That's why I'm so excited now to live here where my dream has come true. She's standing next to you, Mike."

"I think you're really blessed, Marcia, to have a son like this, who's excited about horses. Some call it a curse, but it builds a person's character."

"Thank you, Mike. I'm glad you could share this with us."

She winked at me, "Okay both of you, you guys have a horse standing there. I'm going to the house, and I'll leave you alone."

CHAPTER 13

Momma and Baby

I woke with a start with the reminiscent memories of Mom, Mike, Miya, and me still fresh on my mind. I realized I had drifted off to sleep at about 2:00 a.m. It had been a long night.

I felt like I needed to go out to the barn to see if the little bay colt had all his first milk or colostrum and was standing up strong. I jumped into some old dirty sweats. I prepared a batch of hot bran mash for the mare, it would be great, I thought, after that long ordeal of foaling that big leggy colt. I grabbed a cup of hot chocolate. Just out the back door, my dog Jake met me, and we hurried to the barn. Jake began wagging his tail as we got to the stall. That seemed to be a good sign. I peered over the stall wall. There was this big gangly colt standing there looking up at me wagging his tail with milk all over his face. Momma mare was busy eating some hay. All looked well, and I quietly went into the stall and gave her the bran mash. Now to find two things. One was the afterbirth I had set aside. I knew how important it was. Being a veterinarian, I could take care of any problems. Retaining anything inside of her was big trouble for the mare. Just one piece of the afterbirth retained inside would cause an infection that could be very detrimental to the new mother, I unraveled it and laid it out on the straw. The afterbirth is really two things. It's the placenta, which was attached to the inside of the uterus, and the amnion, which encapsulates the foal. The foal is attached to the umbilical cord which is the source of nutrients provided by the mare through the placenta. When he emerges from the mare, he breaks the sack of the amnion with his front hooves making it possible for him to take his first breath of life. He literally goes out of the sack of the amnion with the umbilical cord still attached. As the mare and new foal rest, the placenta pumps the remaining blood through the umbilical cord into the foal. It isn't long until either Momma mare or new foal moves or stands, separating the umbilical cord from the foal at the navel. What's left hanging out of the mare is the amnion and umbilical cord with the placenta still attached to the uterus of the mare. If all goes well, the placenta will detach itself from the uterus. The afterbirth, which is the combination of the amnion, umbilical cord, and placenta, will gradually fall to the ground, from the birth canal of the mare, turning the placenta inside out. So far, so good. No holes or pieces were missing out of it. It looked like all the afterbirth was complete. As I looked under her tail, I didn't see any swelling or tearing of the vulva. Now I needed to see if I could find the meconium that would pass as a first bowel movement from the foal. Last night, before I went to bed, I gave the baby an enema to encourage the passing of that meconium, the last remnants of what's left inside the baby's tummy before it ingests any milk from its mother. It's an almost molasses like, sticky blob with three or four clumps. Usually the babies are a little constipated. It looked like Momma's also had a bowel movement. That's good. There's the meconium. There was one more thing I needed to do.

"Momma, may I touch your baby?"

Momma looked around at me and nuzzled the colt, reassuring all of us that it was okay. Crouching down to one knee, gently reaching out, touching the new foal so as not to startle him, I wrapped my arms around his little chest and hips, calming the foal as I gently looked in his mouth for a possible cleft palate, noting that it was perfect. I then looked at his navel stump.

"Let me apply a little tincture of iodine on your navel to protect you against infection."

The navel is a temporary passageway for pathogens that could lead to deadly consequences for the newborn foal.

"Wow, I bet that stung. Momma, your teats look good. The baby has been nursing."

This morning in February certainly had a chill in the air. I sat there looking at this special broodmare and new colt with so much gratitude and emotion in my heart. What an adventure had brought this mare into our lives. This foal, a co-creation with God, represented a new chapter in everybody's life. I shed a tear and thanked God for the gifts of life in front of me.

CHAPTER 14

The Nature of Horses

"Mathew, did you take care of that assignment I gave you?" asked Mike.

"Oh, you mean sitting in the stall or paddock with Miya and writing down everything that I saw and experienced? Well, you know Mike, it was hard just sitting there and not doing anything. She just ignored me at first, but after a while, she came right up to me looking at me saying, 'Well what are you gonna do now?' But I just sat there, like you said. She sniffed me. What I did notice was that she felt more comfortable with me. It was like we came to an agreement that we are stuck here together, and we might as well make the best of it." I snickered. "Oh, I met this girl down at the Grange Hall at the community meeting. Her name is Shirley, and she has horses. She's a member of the 4-H club, and she invited me to be a member. I asked her to come over the other day to help me. She helped me put on the halter and brush her and clean out her feet. I've been so anxious to get up and brush her. Was it okay that I touched her? Because one time she nudged me and pushed me over. I didn't even see her there. She just came up behind me and did that. I was in there cleaning the paddock."

"I think she wants to have company, Mathew. This might be a good opportunity for me to teach you about the nature of horses. Did you notice that when Miya was out there and something scared her or she saw something in the distance, how she reacted?"

"I did see that one time. There were some coyotes in the distance. That's a little scary to me. We never saw coyotes down in the city. But here off in the distance at night, I hear those critters yapping."

"Why do you think you get scared?"

"I don't want to get attacked by coyotes and get eaten."

"Coyotes are called predators Mathew. They eat other living things. Rabbits, squirrels, cats, dogs, whatever they can get a hold of. And they will eat horses also. Now if you're one of those little things that got eaten by coyotes, what do you think you might want to do?"

"I'd do everything in my power to keep from being eaten," I said.

"Critters that get eaten by predators are called prey animals. In Africa, have you seen all those photos of lots and lots of animals off in the plains together in those groups? There's safety in numbers within the herd."

"I see. In school, it was always nice when I had my friends around me for protection from the bullies."

"Yeah, at least there, they don't want to eat you I hope," joked Mike.

"Well, getting back to Miya. Think of her as an animal that could be eaten. Now if you are going to be eaten. You would probably want to look out for danger or all the other animals that might want to eat you, right?"

"Yes, I can see that."

"The way that prey animals react to danger is by running away from it, but if they have to, they'll stand and fight those predators. In numbers, all the horses want is safety, and once they're safe, they can eat. That's really important. The next thing they can do without worries is to have fun, and they have less to worry about when they are with you. Keeping into consideration the horse's point of view, you can then appreciate how they react to the world. Now think of it, you are a predator, Mathew. I bet you like that pork chop every night?"

"I sure do. Mom makes a good pork chop."

"Well, that pork chop came from a prey animal. We always have to think about how we react too, Mathew. A hunter, be it a man or a predator, would carefully approach his target, and when he got close to it, he would pounce on it and hold it down. A horse, on the other hand, is going to notice that creeping monster coming after him and run away. If he's in a herd, he's going to warn his neighbors, and they'll all run away. But if that predator was really close they'll stop and actually fight that predator. I know Mathew, this is a little bit much for you, but it's very important to understand as you start to work with Miya."

"I think I understand what you're talking about Mike."

"The next assignment I have for you Mathew is to consider what I've mentioned about the relationship between predator and prey. In other words, you and Miya. All Miya wants, above all else, is to be safe. Now that the heavy part is done, I can help you with the easy part, that fence."

"Thanks, Mike."

I looked up from the fence we were working on to see my mom bringing out refreshments. She must have thought we deserved a break from our hard work.

"Thanks, Mom," I said.

"Thanks, Marcia. This sure quenches our thirst. We could almost jump into the irrigation canals about now."

"Hey Mom, you know that pork chop that we had last night is from a prey animal." I chuckled.

Mom laughed. "What have you been teaching this young man Mike."

"Well you know us meat eaters are building up a pretty good appetite out here. Even little Miya is looking pretty good to us, that little pork chop." We all laughed together.

"Speaking of an appetite. I went ahead and made some good food for you guys when you're finished."

"Thanks, Marcia. Your son is a hard worker. You should be proud of him."

"I'll see you guys inside."

"We'll both be in in a little bit, once we feed the girl."

Years later, Mike would share some of his most intimate moments with me. This helped me get into his mind. Where he was coming from. Up before the sun, Mike would be outside inspecting his truck getting ready for another run as he contemplated the prior day's activities. Mike had told me he thought about how much fun he'd had with Miya, but he knew he still had to make a living. He's told me it was another day and he was still alive, and he was so thankful for that. There were so many days that Mike had wanted to drive off a cliff. He'd realized that depression just sits on you like a big old monster that won't move off. Mike often told himself that he was going to make it. The sun was coming up over the horizon. Besides, what a breath of fresh air it is to be with a horse again. Mike's thoughts would drift to the times when on an off-ramp on the freeway, there would be mares with their foals right there in the field next to the road. Stopping, he would get out and go up next to the fence and beckon the foals to come over to visit. That would jolt him back to the good old times. Horses really were Mike's salvation. He often told himself he must have courage, and that refrain would enter his mind when he found himself down emotionally. Mike wondered if that still small voice was God speaking to him. By this time, automatically, Mike said he had mounted his truck, and off he went to the hay producer down the road to load the big truck and trailer with the precious cargo for the dairy cattle up in Washington.

CHAPTER 15

A Playday I'll Never Forget

Oh, how many times I have cherished the memories of my youth. Like after the 4-H meeting at the Grange Hall when Shirley and I were in the barn fitting the saddle and bridle on Miya.

Shirley said, "Since we have this saddle on Miya, do you want to get on her?"

"You think I can?"

"Sure I'll help you. I'll hold her. She looks like she's already been trained to ride but just in case, I'll be there to hold on. Miya is a fairly tall horse but you, being a tall, lanky boy, should have no problem stepping up into the stirrup. Now be real quiet. Before you get on, talk to her, and ask her, 'Can I get up there?'"

"Okay. I will." Miya turned around and looked at me as if to say, sure it's okay. "This is the first time I've ridden on a real horse and not a rental horse."

"Okay, Mathew when you step up there, I just want you to stand in the stirrup. That's all and just talk to her. Since I'm holding her, everything's okay. Later on, I'll show you how to get on her by yourself safely. There, how does that feel when you're standing there?" asked Shirley.

"Wow! This is neat," I said.

"Okay, now talk to her. Look right in her eye and ask her, 'Can I get up the rest of the way?' When you get that answer from her, go ahead and put your foot over the saddle and gently put your foot into the other stirrup. There, you did that great, Mathew."

"Oh this is great. I'm actually sitting on my girl with a saddle."

"She's pretty quiet. How old did you say she was?"

"She is eight years old."

"I know that just a couple weeks ago she was down at the auction yard with all those other horses. We need to take it a little bit easy with her right now until she gets in condition. I'll just walk around a little bit, so you can get used to being on top of her."

"Shirley, are you taking your horse this Saturday to the play day?"

"Yes, I am."

"Would it be okay if Miya and I hitched a ride with you?"

"Sure, I'll ask my parents. We have a big enough trailer. About tonight … it is only a business meeting, so you can meet all the kids and their parents, but Saturday will be Miya's first day to be introduced to everybody. There's going to be a lot of other kids from all over the area there with their horses. This is a regional 4-H play day. We better get over to the meeting."

Everyone was curious who that new boy was as I walked in the door of the meeting.

Our 4-H leader got our attention. "Everybody. I want you to meet Mathew Peters who lives down on Walker Road. He's new to 4-H and has never had a horse before."

I then realized that I was the only boy in the club with all those girls. How lucky can a boy be?

"Shirley, there aren't many boys here."

"Yeah, boys like their motorcycles better." René chimed in. "Yep, and they're out there killing themselves riding those bulls. They just want to be rodeo cowboys."

Carly asked curiously, "Don't you want to be a rodeo cowboy?"

"Really Carly. I don't even know what rodeo cowboys do. Where I'm from, I lived close to a horse racetrack. I would go to the morning workouts and watch the horses run around the tracks. My sister would tell me that she just went there to hang out back in the barns and smell the horses. I thought that was kind of funny, but really there's something to it. I really like the smell of horses."

In unison, most of the girls there agreed.

"Okay kids, come on, sit down. Let's get this meeting to order." Mrs. Brown was our 4-H leader. She was the mother of one of the girls at the meeting. Carly's older sister was the assistant 4-H leader. She was planning to go to college for pre-veterinary. The order of the day was to elect officers and prepare for the play day on Saturday. My mind was reeling with all the new things I was learning. It was especially fun with all these girls.

Early Saturday morning, Shirley's parents drove into the driveway. I ran outside to greet them, guiding them back to the barn. I was up until midnight cleaning my saddle and bridle. Miya was all cleaned up and ready to go. She had already been fed. I was so excited, I couldn't even sleep. Mom came out to make sure everything was okay. She went over to Miya and scratched her before Shirley's dad loaded her into the trailer. "You be a good girl for Mathew."

I gave Mom a big hug.

Mom said, "You be sure to be kind to her."

"I will, Mom."

The other horses whinnied at Miya, and she willingly loaded into the trailer.

"Bye, Mom! I'll see you later this evening."

It was a twenty-mile trip over to the fairgrounds in Redmond. The parking lot was full of horse trailers with hundreds of boys and girls with their horses preparing for the day's events. I had never seen so many horses in one place before. The plan was for me to saddle Miya and just ride around and get used to being with so many riders and horses. Out of the corner of my eye, I saw one boy being rough with one of his horses.

"What is he doing, Shirley?" I asked

"I know that boy, Mathew. His father is a cowboy. They own a big cattle ranch over in Prineville. Not every cowboy is like this, Mathew, but you may see this happen. Our 4-H leaders discourage this. Some of these boys are hard headed. My parents have always told us to be very kind to our horses."

With Shirley's help, I mounted Miya, and we rode off to the arena.

A group of boys on their horses came riding over and said, "Who's this new kid Shirley?"

"This is Mathew, everybody."

"Is that one of those squirrelly Arabians?" they asked.

All the other boys were riding quarter horses.

I said "Yes, she is an Arabian. What do mean 'squirrelly'?"

They just laughed and rode away. I started feeling a little bit self-conscious. I didn't know the boys yet.

"What do they mean, Shirley, about being squirrelly?"

"That's is something that people don't understand about Arabian horses. They think that they're just nuts."

"Miya is not nuts. She's really nice," I said.

Shirley had an event to ride in. I rode over to the fence and waited for her. Standing next to me were the same boys that commented earlier about my Arabian.

I wanted to be friends with some boys, so I struck up a conversation with them.

"I'm from L.A. I just moved up here two months ago."

They seemed friendly enough. I remembered Shirley saying something about the rodeo, so I struck up a conversation.

"Do you guys do rodeo?"

"Sure. Every Saturday there is cattle roping down at the roping arena. They do team penning and heading n' heeling."

"Wow," I said. "That sounds interesting."

"You want to come down sometime?" said one of the boys.

Just then Shirley rode up. "Mathew, did you see my go?"

"I'm sorry Shirley I was busy talking to these boys."

"I'm going again in a couple minutes. Make sure you watch me then. Okay?"

"All right."

I watched attentively while Shirley was swerving in between a bunch of poles out there in the arena. Swerving in and out down to the end and coming back again. That horse was amazing. I wonder if I can do that with my horse sometime, I thought. Shirley came out of the arena and ran up to me, sliding to a stop. The dust billowing all over.

"Well, how did you like that?"

"That was amazing," I said as I choked on the dust.

"Follow me, Mathew."

Turning her horse sharply. I followed and noticed that Miya turned just as sharp. I was surprised that I was able to hold on so well. I wasn't even holding onto the saddle horn anymore. Arriving at the barrel racing arena, we stopped and watched attentively as one horse after another traveled around three barrels in the middle of the arena.

"This is a timed event," said Shirley. "They have to start at one end of the arena. Watch how they go around that first barrel, okay. And then around the next barrel. Did you notice she knocked that down? They're not supposed to knock the barrels down. When they go around that barrel there's one barrel left, then they go as fast as they can to where they started from."

"That's amazing. Look how fast they're going, and they're not coming off."

"You can do this someday, too. There's a lot to learn in order to do that properly. Now watch this boy."

"What are those things on their heels?" I asked

"Oh, those are spurs."

"Spurs? What are they for? That must hurt. And that guy is just slamming those things into the horse's side."

"Now keep on watching," said Shirley, trying to change the subject.

I have a lot to learn, I thought.

It was late when the horse trailer pulled into the little farm on Walker Road. I was bushed, and I was sure that Miya was also. Shirley's horse was already dropped off. I quickly unloaded the saddle, bridle, and equipment. By this time, I was able to unload Miya all by myself. "Thank you, Mrs. Anderson, for taking us. I sure enjoyed myself."

"You're welcome, Mathew. It was nice to have you. You're welcome to do this again sometime. Since you don't have a horse trailer, we'll be glad to take you."

Just then, Mom came out of the house and handed Mrs. Anderson a big bag of cookies and thanked her for her kindness.

"How did things go?" Mom asked me.

"It was amazing. I actually rode Miya the whole time, and she was wonderful. She didn't even try to buck me off. I've seen so many movies where cowboys are out there with their horses bucking all around. Not Miya. She was perfect. And Shirley, you'll want to see how she rides her horse in so many events. She's so talented, Mom. I met a lot of other boys. They invited me to go to the arena every Saturday night for some special events. It's just down the road. I could ride Miya down there."

"Well, just make sure that you are safe. I don't want you or Miya to get hurt."

"Mom, it's okay. Don't worry."

"You take care of your girl and come on in for some supper. You look beat."

"I sure am, Mom. I'll be in the little bit."

CHAPTER 16

A Mother's Love

My mom had some time to herself on Saturday. This gave her an opportunity to update Mrs. Chapman over in the valley about her son Michael. "Hello, Mrs. Chapman. This is Marcia over in Alfalfa."

"Hi, Marcia. Did you get to see my son?"

"We did. Mike came home from one of his trips and came over to help us with our new horse again. His whole attitude has changed. He seems a lot happier. He did tell us that he was having a hard time, but he didn't go into great detail. There was a big surprise though. Evidently, the mare that we rescued was familiar to him. That's why he got so emotional. Our horse came from one of his horses."

"That explains so much."

"There was such a contrast from the other day,". explained Mom.

"I'm so happy to hear this. I thought it might be a good idea to give you the phone number of one of Mike's old friends. Maybe you two can get together."

"Thank you, Mrs. Chapman. Go ahead and give him my number. He can call me."

"As usual, if there are any other bits of information concerning Mike, keep me informed."

"Goodbye, Mrs. Chapman."

CHAPTER 17

Mike's Overdue Visit

For Mike, there was really a routine two-day trip. But this time there was a back haul that delayed his return by another day. After the delivery in Tillamook, the route back to Central Oregon would take him close to his parent's home. Now as he rumbled down the road a spark of life that was gone started to return. Mike had been embarrassed to visit his parents. Dark thoughts had dominated his life for so long. Thinking of that horse across the street had given him hope to return home, instead of an empty house, and Mathew was so much like his son. There was light at the end of the tunnel.

The rural scene in Dallas, Oregon situated in the central part of the Willamette Valley loomed in front of Mike. The pastures with lush green grass rushing by his window reminded him of his own happy days at his ranch in the Tualatin Valley, west of Portland. Surprising himself, Mike shook his head. He remembered. This was the best he'd felt in years. His mom and dad's home was nestled up on top of the hill west of Salem, Oregon. The view of the Willamette River and the Cascade Mountains in the distance welcomed his gaze. His dad was a retired marine major and his mother, retired from the navy, a woman accepted for volunteer emergency service (WAVES), as they called them back then. Both in their nineties, still energetic, they were quick to remind him with humor that all in his family wear their genes well. His mom told the story about her dad who was a count from the province of Florence, Italy. "Count DiCoaciello. When my Grandpa died, my sister, the eldest named Took, inherited the title of Countess. I was now the Countess DiCoaciello, being the only living heir," she'd said. She told Mike that he was next in line. Mike was conceived in Italy, but his 25 percent Italian was all that he had to qualify for that title. Mike turned on to the road leading to the top of the hill. The road circled the scenic hilltop. The wide spot in the road that he so often passed on his way to their house appeared. The big truck fit perfectly in that spot. With hesitation, Mike pulled over and whispered a prayer. "Heavenly father. I'm so thankful for such a loving family. Parents who care for me. I'm thankful that you allowed us to come together. Please help me to lift my spirits. Give me strength. Bless my Mom and Dad. In Jesus name, amen." Mike got out and walked up to the house. The front porch light was on. Responding to a knock on the door, the familiar voices inside came to life.

"I'll get it, dear."

His Dad opened the door. A look of surprise and then a hearty smile came over his face. Mike just looked at him for a couple seconds.

"Hi, Dad," said Mike.

"Well son, you're a sight for sore eyes."

That still, strong hand reached out and grasped his son joyfully.

"I'm sorry, Dad, I haven't seen you in so long," uttered Mike.

Holding Mike at arm's-length, his Dad looked long and deep into Mike's eyes.

"I knew you'd return someday. Come on in. Your Mom is going to be so surprised and happy to see you."

A sweet voice from around the corner in the kitchen filled the air.

"Who's that dear?"

Drying her hands with a dish towel, Mike's Mom rounded the corner. A look of temporary disbelief was followed by outstretched arms and a smile that made an aged face come to life with a sparkle. Tears began to flow as mother and son embraced.

"I miss you guys so much," Mike said, the words came flowing out amid the tears. They both went over and sat on the sofa looking at each other, wiping away the tears with the dishtowel. His dad took his place on the big comfortable chair by the fireplace.

His Mom spoke up, "Mike, we've been so worried about you. You're strong. Remember what we always told you to 'have courage?' Our prayers have always been directed your way. We always thought you needed to go through this grieving. I know loss is something that hits people strongly in different ways. The loss of your sister thirty years ago to cancer and your brother to alcoholism hit all of us very hard. Our faith in God helped us all through those days and will help us now Mike."

"Mom, my feelings that all this was my fault have dominated my thinking for a long time. You and Dad always counseled me to be true to myself. You know how hard-headed I am."

His Mom smiled at him, nodding her head.

"Mom, I'm starting to come out of the fog that has shadowed me. I'm learning to forgive myself and others. Those things I found were holding me back for so long in my life have been replaced by positive forces. Something unexpected happened about a week ago. Some neighbors of mine over in Alfalfa rescued a mare from the killer buyer at the local auction. The Peters is their name. They have a son named Mathew. One day, he came running over asking me for some tools to help get the place ready for a horse that they just bought. 'Do you want to come over and see her?' he'd said. You know me, how I love my horses. 'You have a horse, huh?' I said. It seemed intriguing to me, and I accepted his invitation."

Mike's Mom eagerly listened to what Mike had to say. Having been aware of this for some time because of the conversation with my Mom, over in Alfalfa. She thought it was wise not to say anything. She thought to herself that this was the answer she had been praying for.

"Mike, are you going to stay for supper?"

"I would love to. But I have to get back over to Central Oregon. This was a great opportunity for me to stop on my way back from Tillamook."

His Dad got up from his comfortable chair and joined Mike and his Mom at the door.

"Don't make yourself a stranger, son. Your Mom and I are always praying for you. Have courage and be kind."

"I love you," his Mom said as she showed him out the door.

He hugged them both and whispered, "I love you, too."

CHAPTER 18

That Squirrelly A Rab

It was late when Mike pulled into his driveway. The night was hot and balmy. There was no sign of life in Mike's house except for the light on the front porch. It seemed peaceful. Mike noticed there was a light on in the barn and though that I might still be in the barn taking care of Miya. Mike parked his truck and walked across the street. The light was on in the house, so he went ahead and knocked on the door.

"Hello, Mrs. Peters; it's Mike from across the street. Anybody home?"

Mom opened the door and greeted Mike.

"You've been gone for a while," said Marcia. "Mathew is out in the barn spending some time with his girl. Why don't you go out there and say hi to them? He would love to see you."

Opening the door to the barn, Mike peeked in to see me lying on the hay next to the stall. The door was open, and Miya was eating hay next to me. I looked up surprised.

"Mike, hi there I have so much to tell you."

"Look at her," said Mike. "You don't need a fence for her. She doesn't want to leave your side."

"I know, Mike. I love her so much."

Mike rubbed his hands through her coat, commenting that I had done a wonderful job grooming her.

"Did you learn about grooming at 4-H? Your girl is looking wonderful."

"Not only that, but last weekend I went to the play day with Miya. My friend Shirley picked me up in her big trailer. I met a lot of kids with their horses. I didn't realize there were so many types of horses. Quarter horses, thoroughbreds, some little kids with ponies, and I even saw some big huge horses they call draft horses. All I did was ride Miya. She was so good. Shirley's horse was in many events. That horse is fast. She went in pole bending, barrel racing, something called keyhole where she runs down and turns around in this little spot marked with white lines on the ground and then runs as fast as she can back to the other side of the arena. That was amazing. I was so anxious to ride Miya. But I was good; you don't have to worry about me. There was one thing that worried me. You know, Miya is my first horse, and she is so nice to me. When I got to the fairgrounds, I looked over and there was a boy that was beating on his horse. I don't understand what he was doing, but the horse wasn't very happy. The same boy joined some others and came up to me a little bit later and looked at my horse and said, 'Oh, you're on that squirrelly Arabian.' That really bothered me, Mike. What do they mean by squirrelly? He was on what he said was a quarter horse. Is there a difference between a quarter horse and an Arabian?"

Mike laughed.

"There's something that you probably will learn, and now is a good time for me to share it with you. This might help you. Have you ever noticed that people who think they know a lot about something will just talk and talk and talk and make themselves look really foolish? And all the time you think to yourself, this guy doesn't know anything. I believe that there is a lack of knowledge people have about Arabians. The Arabian horses came from the deserts of the Middle East. They are one of the oldest breeds in the world. The Bedouin of the desert cherished these horses. They were so valuable because they carried them and their families around in the desert. The Arabians were hearty little animals that, even though they were very small, have characteristics that have made them one of the strongest breeds of horses for their size in the world. They have dense bones and the skeletal structure that carries two-thirds of their weight with no problem. They can go in the desert for long periods of time on very little water and food. Their lung and heart capacity surpass that of regular horses. Those boys don't realize, the reason why they call the Arabian horse squirrelly is because they don't understand them. The Arabian horse is very intelligent, very sensitive, and kind. They will devote themselves to their master and would give up their lives to protect them. The Bedouins used to allow their precious mares inside their tents with their children as babysitters. The mares would take part in caring for the young of the tribe. The mare was a treasured possession, cherished so much by the tribe. They would take their mares into battle with them because they would not call out to the other horses giving themselves away like stallions do. They were very brave and protective of their masters. I'll bet you those boys don't even know that the Arabian horse was influential in developing the very horses that they were sitting on. Most light breeds of horses in the world come from the Arabian horse. That boy said that your girl is squirrelly huh? By now, Mathew, you've probably noticed how intelligent your girl is and how sensitive she is. There's a big responsibility. An intelligent horse needs an intelligent master. I'm sorry to say, but those boys probably are riding on horses that are able to take the kind of abuse that that boy was giving to his horse. No horse deserves that. If that were done to your girl, that boy would not have been able to ride her for very long. Your girl needs someone who can discuss and bargain with her. In other words, an intelligent conversation."

"You mean you can talk to your horses?"

"Well, yes, of course, they have their own language. Now the first assignment that I gave you, I asked you to observe. Tell me what you saw."

"Well, she didn't talk to me, but I did notice that when I would call her she would move her ears toward me. With those big eyes, she would look at me, her nose would wiggle when I would scratch her in that certain place that she liked."

"Mathew, you think that was her talking to you?"

"Yes, I can see that."

"There's a thing called body language. Horses communicate with their bodies. Watch their ears; their eyes and their muzzle move with expression, also. They use their tail and stomp their feet. That's why I asked you to sit and watch because you can learn so much. I've learned not only to listen to their noises but also to watch what their slight movements are telling me. Often, I will watch them closely and concentrate. Do you know that they talk to me in pictures? The first thing I see in my mind is a picture of what they're telling me. So, I've learned to talk to them right back in pictures."

"Wow, Mike. I'm just blown away. Where did you learn all this?"

"I have lived with horses now for fifty years. You hang around them for so long that you just absorb this. I also noticed more now, in my life, that I sense the little imperceptible messages that they're giving me. I think it's a gift from God." We both looked at Miya who just let out a big snort. "Really Mike. Look at Miya in there, is she talking to us?"

We laughed.

"Mike, my mom has always told me to be kind. Those boys were so rough with their horses. I noticed that they had long spurs, so called, on their heels and whips. They would take them in the arena and jab those things into their side and just whip them to make them go faster. All I saw were unhappy horses. They had their ears pinned back with their tails swishing."

"Well, Mathew, I think you're more advanced than you think. Because what you are seeing was the body language from those horses."

"I'm just so different from those boys."

"There's so much for you to learn; you've just begun. But you're fortunate that you have this gift inside of you. You said your mother always told you to be kind. That is great wisdom that will take you a long way in your life. Turning to Miya with a caress and looking into two big eyes, Mike breathed into Miya's nostrils, "your little Miya is very precious," Mike said so I could hear him and savor the moment. "It's late, and I have been on the road for a long time. I'm going to wish you and Miya a good night."

"Good night, Mike. I'll see you again soon?"

"Definitely. Take care of that girl. Bye."

While we were in the barn, Mom had gotten a phone call from Mrs. Chapman over in the valley. Mrs. Chapman wanted to pass on the information that she had Mike's friend. Mrs. Chapman asked Mom to give him a call sometime, and that he would be expecting her call. She shared with Mom that Mike had stopped by their house in Salem. She mentioned that his spirits were much better and that they were so happy to see him. Mrs. Chapman told Mom that she never told Mike about our conversations.

"I understand," said Mom. "Probably a good idea that he doesn't know that we've been conversing."

Thanking each other, they pledged to keep in touch.

I walked into the living room where Mom was sitting reading a book. Putting it down,

She mused, "Mathew, you look like a dog just drug you in."

I had straw stuck in my hair, and my shirt was untucked.

"I know, Mom. I've been out there lying in the hay with my little Miya. Mike was at the barn. We had a long conversation. Do you know that the Arabian horse is the oldest breed of horse in the world? Most horses that I saw at the play day came from the Arabian horse. They came from the desert in the Middle East. Mike has a lot of knowledge.

Some boys at the 4-H play day were teasing me about Miya being an Arabian. Mike said that she's special."

Mom agreed.

"How lucky we're friends with Mike. What a coincidence he lives across the street and Miya came about because of him."

"I sure am, Mom. I wish Dad were here. I need to call my sister."

"That's right. We'll call Marion tomorrow."

"Well, good night Mom. I'm gonna take a hot bath and hit the sack."

CHAPTER 19

Mike's Epiphany

For Mike, the mental stimulus with my horse was a brief respite to his daily routine of driving that big truck. He welcomed the little detours. Feeling rejuvenated, he would reminisce the good times and how life had become easier to bear. His excursions into Canada usually added two more days to his routine driving through the Bitterroot Mountains of Idaho and crossing into Canada through the scenic mountain route. Hay production in Canada had decreased demanding product from the fertile volcanic soils in the valleys of Central Oregon. Mike enjoyed driving through Banff that would eventually take him into the Great Plains of Canada.

On these drives, Mike's mind would wander. He had plenty of time later to share with me what went through his mind as he drove through God's creation.

Mike told me he remembered reading books about the Arabian horse in his youth. *The Black Stallion* and *Drinkers of the Wind*, stories that stimulated his imagination. He often thought he was destined to be with those glorious creatures that God created. Mike was unsure if these were just wild imaginations of youth or if he had a destiny. Mike felt a calling. All the important horses that ever came into his life seemed to have been heaven sent. Mike knew that the people he knew in his youth would dismiss those feelings as just follies.

As a boy, his family being in the military, moved many times. Mike's father was distant, and Mike was very close with his mother. He had many unresolved problems that flared up in fits of anger. Mike did not have the blessing of a mentor when he was young, someone who would guide him through these emotional rants. When he was nineteen, he had been employed by a wonderful Arabian breeder in Chico, California. He worked there for five years and that had helped him tremendously. John was a wonderful mentor and attempted to share with Mike the benefit of hard work and self-control. John helped Mike with the way he dealt with his horses and issues of life.

Mike had a problem, though; he thought he was the master of his life, and there was no compromise. The Arabian horse ranch where he had worked in the McKenzie River Valley in Oregon was a turning point in his life. No longer was Mike traveling to see the world, he was in one place for two years living around Arabian horses and learning their language. He emulated the successful trainers in the Arabian horse industry. Monthly subscriptions to the *Arabian Horse World* magazine were devoured from cover to cover. At Arabian horse shows, hovering around big trainers, Mike learned their wares: grooming techniques, training, care, and upkeep. Their halter training techniques intrigued him. Mike saw horses being well cared for and handled with respect, but on the other hand, he saw submission by using the whip and other abusive practices. The contrast conflicted Mike. He had unresolved anger issues with the need to always be in control. His innate voice told him to be kind, so he experimented with various training techniques on the McKenzie River ranch. Little did he know then, that this conflict would set him up for a showdown in the future. Who was he? Will who he was becoming be his downfall? Or would he take the risk to be truthful, standing for principle instead following the ways of the world?

The conflict Mike experienced in the Arabian horse industry moved him to change direction temporarily. He left his beautiful horses at the

McKenzie River to return to school and pursue a veterinary degree. He thought he could provide for the horse's physical well-being instead. After all the work he did, three years later, after bringing up his grade point average to a level that would qualify him for veterinary school, Mike ran out of money. One of the biggest mistakes of his life was to abandon his goal of becoming a veterinarian. His only choice was to go back to transporting horses, and he would transport some of the most famous Arabian horses and hobnob with owners and trainers. This gave Mike a renewed desire to raise his own Arabian horses.

During his time transporting horses for the big movers of the industry, he was chosen to haul a famous Arabian stallion. This stallion's trainer was an up and coming star of the industry. Mike followed his exploits closely and traveled to shows taking notes of his techniques. Mike's mind was set to emulate this successful trainer. He had dreams of stardom.

In the early years, Arabian horses were shown quietly. The halter classes were similar to the classes in 4-H programs where the horses were stood up square and shown to the judge for their genetic breeding potential. In other words, were they put together properly for an athletic function that reflected the traits and standards of the Arabian breed. A change started to occur. The Arabian horse was known for its high spirit and beauty at liberty with its arched neck, high tail carriage, floating trot, and flared nostrils. That look became a desired quality of the Arabian halter horse. Some enterprising handlers came up with techniques that would elicit these qualities from their animals. Unfortunately, in order to accomplish this, the natural instincts of the horse, which is that of a prey animal, fight and flight, were exploited. The predators that we were would control the explosion that occurred delicately. The handler would purposely frighten the horse by shaking a plastic bag or use a whip for intimidation to elicit this behavior. Not every owner or handler of a horse would follow these practices. Some owners and handlers refused to transition into this kind of abuse to win. Judges soon preferred this animated stance over the showmanship stance. The industry started to change. The natural mystique of the Arabian horse and its popularity started to gain strength. The Arabian horse soon became a status symbol. The competition became intense with wealthy individuals and people with dreams of owning the desert Arabian horse. Handlers would clash with their varying techniques of halter presentation in order to please the judges. The price of the Arabian horse would soar with its popularity, their demand was very high. Individuals, including Mike, would get caught up into this maelstrom, with dreams of breeding the exotic Arabian horse. Breeders would dedicate their lives to this goal. Unfortunately, the win at all cost tendencies would start to show their destructive courses. Beloved family horses would come home from their trainers completely changed.

Mike's mother started a new business in Portland, Oregon. She was overwhelmed and needed help. Mike answered the call and devoted himself to helping his mother grow her business. Soon he had opened his own store in Beaverton, Oregon, which became successful rather quickly. His dream of raising his own Arabian horses and showing them soon became a reality. A property with a small barn and acreage became available and all of Mike's spare time was devoted to building his ranch. Working ten hours a day at his business and coming home to build and care for his growing herd dominated his time. He was the happiest he'd ever been with income to propel his new venture and control his own destiny.

The Arabian horses Mike bred soon came of age. His experience watching the successful trainers and breeders influenced him greatly. He felt like a clumsy newcomer, but soon honed his skills and quickly became competitive. As he grew his breeding program, Mike purchased a very well-bred and beautiful Spanish Arabian stallion, *Zalamero, imported from England. He personally cared for his horses. He loved them dearly. His young Arabian stallion, who had so much potential, soon become a victim of Mike's quest for glory. One day when Mike was tuning up this young stallion, the stallion decided he had enough of Mike's abusive techniques. As a boxer would wait for just that right moment to strike, the stallion lunged at Mike, aggressively biting him on the shoulder, picking him up off the ground. Thrashing him, the stallion dropped Mike and proceeded as a prey animal to instinctively escape his grasp. The stallion was just trying to protect himself. Mike's first reaction, and angry, being the dominant member of this duo, was to reach out and beat the horse with his whip. The horse had nowhere to go. Like a predator, Mike held him, and he was at the end of that lead. Mike thought he was in control. Something happened to him at that moment, which would completely change the direction of his life. The Arabian stallion of his dreams that he loved so much was standing there trembling. Mike was the cause of it. How could he have done that? Awkwardly, Mike reached out and hugged his precious and confused stallion. They both cried together. This event, he vowed, would never occur again. To remind him, Mike still has that big scar on his shoulder. He realized that the still small voice from the time of his youth to be kind, was real. No longer would he attempt to win at all costs, with wages being the destruction of the beautiful minds of the Arabian horse that was so inexplicably connected to him.

The year that followed had been a delicate dance between Mike and his young stallion. Mike learned that they could communicate in a better way without intimidation, utilizing his natural desire to play and express his exuberance. He allowed the stallion to express himself and encouraged him to do so through trust in Mike as a protector and still give him boundaries to instill respect as a leader. He was no longer looking outside for answers. What he needed was to look within for the counsel that was inside his spirit from the beginning. An integral balance, to have courage and be kind and be true to himself.

Mike learned a lot about building a relationship from a young filly named Zestrellita, the result of the first breeding to *Zalamero. Mike was a changed individual. He had nurtured this filly, from the time of her conception, they had an almost telepathic communication while she was inside the womb. He would approach her mother and the foal would wiggle inside.

A good friend and kindred spirit, a real natural horseman, joined forces with him to help change some abusive attitudes of the show ring. For the next three years, Mike would dominate the show ring with their handsome stallions and alternative techniques. Even though he was successful in the show ring, bucking the abusive trends was still difficult. The politics of the time had become hard to penetrate. Ultimately, to succeed in the championship level with his competitive horses would prove challenging. The win at all cost forces would dominate the Regional and Championship classes with its hopes for money and prestige. Mike had invested everything to try to compete with these detrimental forces with one last burst of energy. He devoted the focus of his stallion's training in the performance field. Stock horse or reining would be his venue. The committed gambler that he was, with one last chance, Mike thought the avenue he was pursuing would be free of the politics and the win at all costs attitudes. His stallion was very talented. Mike knew he could win at the national level, so he threw his total bankroll at this. Unfortunately, upon entering that field, Mike realized that those forces were heavily at work as well. He'd become totally disenchanted. Succumbing to his quest to compete and win, it broke him financially and emotionally.

When Mike was very young, his father would watch him skating on the lake in Illinois where they lived. His father would watch him fall down and get right back up. He admired Mike for that quality and would continue to tell him to have courage and get back up. It was hard to get back up this time. A drastic change in direction was about to occur in his life and passion with horses.

Mike's mind returned its focus to the present. He remembered the winding roads leading to Kingsgate and the scenic tour through Banff up into the plains south of Calgary, Alberta that lay ahead. Mike had pushed aside these thoughts for years. God had provided Mike with many opportunities to develop an understanding of the forces that changed his life. In deep thought many times as he drove, he would say; "God, thank you for providing me with avenues and crossroads. Having placed my faith in you and the direction you have in my life, I realize that you are in control. Through these trials and tribulations, I have been strengthened. I have not only to see the world as it is but how it could be." So many times he wanted to escape the trials of life, but he was gaining a new perspective in his life instead. These were distant memories.

With a new appreciation for the blessings in life, he woke up every day and thanked God that he was alive. Gradually, the light in Mike's life was returning. "What did You have in store for me?" Mike asked God. "Who am I? I am just going to be Mike, imperfect? Starting back at zero, take me as I am. I am still learning my trade." The distant memory in his head lingered when God said, "Remember who you are. Will who you are be enough? Will you take the risk to truly be who you are? True to yourself?"

I felt privileged that Mike would share these intimate experiences with me. I would absorb this "can do with courage" attitude from Mike. His encouragement to never give up would profoundly influence me.

CHAPTER 20

Shahwan

During Mike's travels in his horse transport days, many friendships were developed. He would visit large beautiful horse ranches that housed the horses of his dreams. Mike purchased a little Arabian filly that captured his fancy. On his way back from Michigan with this new filly, he stopped in Benbrook, Texas to visit a friend at a popular layover spot. His friend mentioned that there was a married couple from Germany inquiring about any Arabian horses that were stabled there. Coincidentally, they had found the only Arabian, his filly. It was destiny. The mutual love for the Arabian horse had sparked an instant camaraderie with feelings that they had known each other forever, soulmates for sure. Their friendship would grow. Walter and Margit Heuser were employees of Lufthansa Airlines. Dallas was a routine layover for them, with three days between their return trip. He would be sure to try to rendezvous with them often while they were in Dallas.

Walter was born in a little town in Germany. As he grew older, he found himself at the home of his neighbors who had farm animals, especially the horse. He would jump on the horse bareback with no bridle or halter and go galloping around the pasture. He would often fall off and get right back on.

Nothing would bother him. Returning home, his mother would ask, "what have you been doing today?"

"Ah, nothing," Walter would say sheepishly.

His mom would laugh. As Walter grew older, his fascination with horses drew him to the fine horses that lived down the road. Horses with spirit, strong, fine-boned with small ears and dished faces. Their nostrils flared as they ran across the pastures, drinking in the wind. He would find himself by those fences, watching these powerful creatures. He would say to himself, "I want one of those."

In Germany, there was a structured training system of apprentice, journeyman, and master horsemen. This would assure that the time-honored traditions of horsemanship were passed on to the generations. Walter became a master. Soon after college, he found a job with Lufthansa Airlines. This suited Walter because he found himself traveling to the Middle East where the horses that he admired so much in his youth originated. On his layovers, he would spend time with the Bedouins, where he sought out the heritage of the desert Arabian horse. Traditionally, as he disembarked from his airplane, gather up his horses and his camel, he would notice that the Badawi would line the roads in welcome of his return. He had made many friends, close friends that shared his passion for the Arabian horse. One prominent Arab gifted Walter an Arabian filly. The Arab tradition of gift giving is sacred, but you do not give that gift back dishonoring the gift giver, but wisdom was well taken and understood that Walter in his job could not have a horse at home. He gratefully thanked his dear friend who relented and received her back.

Walter made many influential friends in the Arabian community in Germany. As he was having breakfast with a friend, he noticed a commotion in the pasture where a young colt had gotten in with the main herd sire of the farm. This colt was a quarter of the size of the stallion. This brave colt, named Said, would get beaten down, get right back up again and again, until finally, he met his match and literally was throttled over the fence. As they went to this tough colt's aid, Walter was so impressed by his strength and courage that he bought him on site. Walter spent time rehabilitating him and teaching him the basics of life. His inherent strength would become apparent as he grew older. He taught him how to dance like the Bedouins had taught their horses. He taught him the finer points of dressage. The bond between these two was great. Walter was given a promotion in the airline to chief purser. As his responsibilities became greater, he had less time to spend with his cherished Said. With much trepidation, he decided to give his precious Said up to his good friend, Herr Dieckman, who owned many quality Marbach mares. Said was 100 percent Marbach. Marbach State Stud of Germany goes back 500 years and produces and provides the best horse bloodstock for the posterity of the German people.

Walter shared stories with Mike about Said's offspring. He was so proud. One year he said, "Mike, a colt was born that, mark my words, is the best colt that Germany has ever produced." Mike dismissed that as a comment from a proud owner, but this would ultimately prove to be a prophetic statement.

Mike would routinely travel to Dallas to meet with Walter and Margit as their friendship grew. One year he presented Mike with a gift of a saddle he had gotten from Morocco. Walter had a great affection for the Badawi horse breeding tribes he would often visit during his layovers in Egypt. He would share his many adventures with Mike.

Walter called Mike while he was attending his store, telling him of a tragedy that struck the Dieckman family. Their son had been killed in a natural gas explosion. Said's special son Shahwan had to be sold. Shahwan needed to go to Mike only, exclaimed Walter. Mike told him that he was in no position to buy a colt, nonetheless go to Germany and see him and then bring him back to America. Walter continued to tell him that no matter what, this will happen. It was his destiny. Mike wondered, is this something that a man who had lived with the Bedouin in the desert had learned? Walter believed heartily that the Arabian horse was a gift from God.

A series of miracles occurred. A surprise inheritance enabled Mike to wind up on Walter's doorstep. Walter opened the door, smiled, and said, "I knew you would come." That afternoon they were headed on the 400-mile trip to see Shahwan.

Mike walked into the three-year-old colt's stall. He was astonished to find himself looking at the most beautiful Arabian stallion he'd ever seen. His heart jumped as he looked into his eyes and saw his soul mate, the spirit he'd been looking for all his life. This majestic creature reached around and put his muzzle on Mike's hand so gently, allowing him to enter his presence. He had a regal bearing with an aloof demeanor. They knew that they had found each other. A young man from Portland Oregon, who dreamed about Arabian horses all his life, was standing in the presence of greatness. "Could this be happening to me?" With an uncanny acceptance of the reality, Mike proceeded to negotiate the purchase of this fine colt. His family was eager to participate in the purchase which would allow him to allay the expenses that were to follow. Quarantine on both ends, travel by airline, and insurance. He looked into Shahwan's eyes and told him that he was going to America. He was in a trance with the feeling that his dreams were about to be fulfilled.

Those dreams would be dashed. Mike's family notified him, telling him their circumstances had changed, and they could not participate. He was devastated. Mike's personality would not let that stand. Like he did on the frozen lake in Illinois, he got right back up. He traveled the country seeking to find partners to fulfill his dream, to no avail. One by one, he would approach people with his proposal. He would hear comments, like "this colt wouldn't compete over here in America." Or, "I'm not willing to take the chance." He even approached his friend John in Chico. His comments were similar.

John was an international judge and would often travel to shows judging Arabian horses. In the ensuing time, Shahwan was recognized by authorities in the government of Germany dealing with Arabian horses and the registry to be worthy of special recognition. The German government held the future survival of the Arabian horse paramount. Pedigree and quality are important. The future survival of the breed would trump the tendency to pass quality stallions up because of competition, the win at all costs attitude that prevailed in America. These attitudes would often pass up quality stallions in favor of politics. After the failed purchase, the German government stepped in for the Dieckmans and sponsored Shahwan in the time-honored testing that would prove the athletic quality and genetic prowess of the Arabian horse.

Arabian breeding stallions underwent a mandatory judging after three years of age. The placings, based on a numerical placement with seven different factors, were evaluated and considered. The tested stallions would be placed in a stud book. The qualifications that year placed Shahwan at the top of the list in the stud book. Shahwan was crowned champion of Germany.

The next important phase was a testing of his athletic ability and his ability to learn and his trainability. This is called the 100-day test. The participants, untrained stallions of all breeds, would compete. For ninety days, they would be trained in six areas. The last ten days they would be tested in five of the six areas. All breeds of stallions would be tested. Warmblood breeds were usually more talented in these disciplines and possessed greater athletic abilities because of their size and physical makeup; they were more capable of scoring higher in these tests. The Arabian horse is the progenitor of most of these breeds. Arabian stallions are often used as improvement sires for the warm blood breeds to maintain their qualities they inherited from the Arabian. The value of these tests is very important to constantly provide the best stallions for the improvement of the people's horses in Germany. The government ran this system. Before this, Shahwan's sire, Said, was tested and found to be the highest scoring Arabian stallion in his class. Shahwan's older brother Saudi also had the highest score. Shahwan had a challenge to follow in their footsteps.

Shahwan was tested with other breeds in his class. The resultant score was the highest score for any Arabian horse that had ever taken the test in the history of the performance test. The prophetic words of Walter stating, "The finest Arabian stallion Germany has ever produced" was coming to pass. In realization of just what they possessed, Shahwan was entered in the upcoming world championship Arabian horse show in Paris. This was the first time that Shahwan was ever shown in a sanctioned Arabian horse show, other than his licensing and testing. In order to qualify for the ultimate championship in Paris, an Arabian stallion needed to win first place in his class which was for his age level.

Mike's friend John, coincidentally, was one of the judges of this class. He did not know that this was the horse Mike had approached him about. The competition was fierce. A stallion named Charlemagne was head to head with Shahwan in the judges' minds. There were three judges involved, and John was trying hard to lobby the others that Shahwan should prevail and win his class. With the judges' cards in, the tabulation resulted in Charlemagne winning by a hundredth of a point. Because Shahwan did not win the class, he was not qualified to go to the championship class. The next day, Charlemagne was crowned world champion.

In the years that followed, Mike became friends with the owner of Charlemagne. She fondly recalled the intense competition that she experienced that day. She agreed that Shahwan was of high quality. She was actually unsure that her horse would prevail. That speaks tremendously of Shahwan, that close to being world champion.

Later on in America, in conversation with John, Mike asked him about that particular class. Without letting him know, he asked him about his experience. Mike then informed him that the horse that he fought so hard for was actually the horse he had asked for help in purchasing. John was astonished and disappointed.

Shahwan would go on to be top ten in the nation's cup of Europe, placing fifth in the rankings. To this day, Shahwan is honored to be a Century Stallion, one that does not occur but every 100 years. Two years later, after his failed purchase, Mike traveled to Germany with his mother and good friend to try to restore his honor to the breeders of Shahwan. You do not break a promise and remain honorable to a German. Upon visiting Shahwan in Aachen, Germany where he was presented in front of the crowd in a special presentation, Mike was able to rendezvous with Shahwan in the arena before his presentation. He looked into his eyes and promised him that someday they would fulfill their destiny to be together. That occasion has been preserved in a photo that is cherished to this day. The Dieckmans remained his close friends thereafter.

CHAPTER 21

My First Riding Lesson

Shirley agreed to give me riding lessons on Miya. The past weeks of special care and attention for Miya were paying off. What a challenge. Shirley took the saddle and bridle off. With a long line attached to Miya's halter, I was put through some strenuous exercises. With no hands, I was made to reach out and touch her tail and her ears, first at a walk and then at a trot.

"Your aptitude for riding is impressive," commented Shirley.

I reminded Shirley that I had been involved in gymnastics in L.A. "That's why I'm able to stay on."

Smiling, she said, "Okay, smarty-pants. I want you to get on backwards now."

"Sure. No problem," I said.

This time Shirley let Miya out longer on the line and asked her to move out a little bit faster. It was hilarious. I started bouncing uncontrollably and just grabbed onto Miya's butt. Miya gave a little buck, and I went flying to the ground.

"I know that's not fair, Mathew. But believe me, I've been through the same thing with my teacher."

"Let me try that again," I demanded.

"Okay—get up there."

This time I was prepared. There was no change in the tempo this time. Shirley was impressed. Without hesitation, I even changed position and ended up facing forward while Miya was moving.

"You didn't tell me you would go so fast. See, I told you I'm pretty good."

"Okay. This time, take this cup of hot water. I'm going to make you trot, and I don't want a drop of that spilling. This was the first thing my Mom did to me. It really teaches you to be independent and move with your horse."

I proceeded to pass that test. Realizing the water had gotten cold, the next time around, I poured it all over her. Not letting that get the best of her, Shirley reached down and grabbed the hose and drenched both of us. The hot summer days of Central Oregon usually ended up this way with the greatest of water fights with Mom pitching in enthusiastically.

Sitting on the lawn with Miya grazing happily, I mentioned to Shirley that the boys at the play day invited me to go to the roping arena on Saturday.

"That's pretty advanced riding they do over there at the roping arena," said Shirley. "Those Cowboys are very experienced. The quarter horses they ride usually come from the local cattle ranches."

"Have you ever been to one of those Shirley?"

"I have, but I usually just sit on my horse and visit with the girls in our club."

"I'm getting pretty good riding Miya, Shirley. You think that we could go over there sometime?"

"Yeah, that would be kind of fun. It's only about three miles up the road, and we can ride there. That might be a good experience for you to watch how the cowboys handle their horses."

CHAPTER 22

A Valuable Lesson

Saturday afternoon, Shirley met me at my farmhouse with her horse, Barney. We both set out together for the roping arena. Mom had made us a sack lunch. The roping arena was well lit, and the events usually went on till about ten o'clock at night. There was going to be a full moon that night, so riding home would be no problem. Mom promised to drive down and watch since that would be educational for her, and it would give her a chance to socialize with the locals.

Settling in next to the arena fence, I was transfixed watching all the action. The most popular event was the heading and heeling. One cowboy would rope a calf that was let out of the chute, and the other would follow behind and rope the calf's back legs. If they were successful, they would stretch that calf out and the official would drop a flag. It was a timed event. Mom walked up and climbed onto the fence next to us. This was quite a different experience for Miya. Her ears were pricked forward. When the action would get close to the fence, she would back up. I soon learned to hang on. One time, Miya stood there and shook hard. I couldn't believe what was happening and just laughed. Shirley looked over and reassured me. Next was calf roping. Those calves would come out of the chute, the cowboy would rope the calf, jump off a perfectly good horse, go down and pick the calf up, wrestle him to the ground, and tie his feet.

"How do they do that?" I asked with amazement.

"Lots of practice, Mathew," answered Shirley.

Mom excused herself to go off and see if she could find some friends. During a break in the action, the boys noticed us and came riding over. This time they invited us over to the practice arena. They seemed nice this time. Shirley had a look of wariness about her.

Jeb approached and said, "You've got a pretty nice horse. Do you want to race her?"

Being competitive, I said, "Sure.

We lined up and off we went. Jeb's horse took off like a flash. Miya just trotted and loped a little bit.

Jeb returned and laughed. "I told you she's a nice horse. You want to try that again?"

Forgetting everything I had discussed with Mike, I said, "Of course." I looked down and saw one of the boys had spurs on. "Hey, can I borrow those things? Yeah, those spurs."

I quickly put on the spurs as Shirley looked on, saying, "You better be careful Mathew, you really shouldn't."

"It'll be okay. I'm not going to let him beat me."

With the spurs on this time, I lined up. Aiming my horse to the finish line, we both took off. This time, not wanting to be bettered by Jeb, I jabbed those spurs into Miya's side. With great surprise, Miya pinned her ears and bucked wildly throwing me hard to the ground.

Shirley went down and caught Miya who was standing there shaking. Shirley, upon returning, glared at me. "See, I told you so."

I walked up to her and took hold of the reins. The trust that I had built up over these last few weeks had been dashed.

Shirley told me to take off those spurs and give them back. "It's time to go Mathew, but first I want you to walk your girl around. Do you think she's gonna want you to get on now after what you just did?"

I turned all red.

"Now you need to apologize to her before you get back up on her."

This time Shirley had to hold on to Miya while I got back up. Slightly jumpy this time, I had to reassure her that what she perceived was going to happen, indeed will not happen. After about ten minutes, Shirley and I exited the arena and headed home. The moon was bright, and the night was warm. There wasn't any conversation on the return trip. Mom came driving by and slowed down to wave. Thinking that all was okay, she headed home.

Mom greeted us as we rode up toward the barn. "How did it go tonight kids?" Sheepishly, I looked up at Shirley and then told Mom what I had done.

"Oh, Mathew," Mom said.

"Shirley, I'm so sorry," I said. "I feel really bad."

"Don't tell me that. Tell that to Miya."

Those were literally the only words that came out of our mouths since we left the arena. I had a long time to think about what happened on the ride home. Mom thanked Shirley for her help.

"You're welcome, Mrs. Peters."

I looked up and nodded my thanks, realizing just how good of a friend Shirley really was.

"It would be a good idea, Mathew, to get that hose and give her a good rinse," said Shirley. "Spend some time with her, and I'll see you tomorrow, okay."

With that, she and Barney headed home. Mom held Miya while I unsaddled her. I rinsed her with nice, cool water. The moon was high in the sky. Miya settled down and grazed while Mom fetched some snacks out of the house. In the distance, the rumble of a truck grew louder. Miya looked up to see those familiar lights enter the driveway across the street. She went back to eating as Mom and I discussed the events of the evening. I asked Mom not to say anything to Mike about what happened.

"I'll tell him myself. I sure learned a lesson tonight. Mike told me a lot about body language. Miya was sure cussing at me tonight. Look at her now. She's so forgiving."

This day would be stamped into my memory.

CHAPTER 23

Fond Memories

I must have drifted off in the stall. I shook my head and gathered my thoughts about those immature times of my life in Alfalfa. Those days were transformative for me.

Looking around at the fresh new life with its familiar smells, I felt closer to God. "You've always been so good to me God, and now this gift that you've given us. This beautiful colt." I sat in that comfortable straw as the colt curiously chewed on my shoes and investigated my familiar voice. I had visited with him while he was in his mommy's tummy daily during his gestation. A gentle touch would elicit a response. Almost telepathically, the colt would respond and thrash around. At times, I had to calm him down. He was so excited to feel my presence. There is a special connection that had developed. Momma, who had already formed that special bond with me seemed to welcome that interaction. When that big colt was born, he heard his mother's nicker and maneuvered his way in search of her gentle touch. When his needs were quenched, my voice would turn his head again as he looked my way knowingly. Satisfied, the little guy plopped down next to me putting his head on my lap with Mom, proud and contented, looking on.

Oh, I've learned so much from all this, I thought. Where would I be without Mike's influence and continual mentoring for the last twenty years? Being Mike's apprentice in his horsemanship clinics, Mike would often tell me, "Mathew. You are very fortunate to learn now in your life, what took me fifty years to learn. The mantle of horse whisperer was a great honor. To be known as a horse listener rose to a higher level."

Is this the meaning of happiness? Being together with the horses you love? I settled back to my thoughts and continued the journey into my past as the colt snoozed softly on my lap.

CHAPTER 24

Plans for Mike

The phone rang, and Mom answered with a voice on the other end identifying himself as James Reynolds. "Is this Mrs. Peters?"

Mom answered intuitively. "Mrs. Chapman over in the valley said you would call. Are you Mike's old friend?"

"Yes, Mike and I share many things in common. We go back a lot of years. I own a winery over in the Valley and share the love of Arabians with Mike. Mrs. Chapman has told me of your concerns about Mike."

"Yes, Mr. Reynolds, I'm glad we're able to get together. Can I call you James?"

"Of course. Mike's mother told me that she had told you a little bit about Mike's past. She thought it would be better if I shared more of the details to help you understand him a little bit better. If you don't mind, I'd like to do that with you right now. Do you have the time?"

"Sure. I would love to hear what you have to say."

James began his account, which went like this: Mike was so disenchanted with the Arabian horse industry that he decided to go over to Germany and visit his friend Walter. While he was there, he thought it would be a good idea to share the pictures of his band of horses and his stallion *Zalamero with breeders in Germany. Mike had just gotten married, and his new wife was anxious to see that stallion Shahwan. Mike and his wife accompanied Walter to the historical

Castle Eringerfeld that served as the breeding farm for the Dieckmans, the owners of Shahwan.

The famous German stallion had generated revenue to rejuvenate the equestrian quarters of the castle. Mr. Dieckman's son accompanied them around the countryside to see Shahwan's offspring. On one visit, Mike shared photographs of his horses with a local breeder thinking they might be interested in his stallion's offspring, the photograph of *Zalamero came up. Mike was trying to sell his foals. But the German breeder kept on going back to the stallion's photograph. He asked if he was for sale. "Sell him? Never," Mike said. But having experienced his disillusionment with the Arabian industry, he thought to himself, maybe a change of venue might be good. He started to talk to the gentleman about maybe leasing his stallion.

With help from Herr Dieckman's son-in-law as the translator, he negotiated a lease. Astonished by what he had just done, Mike traveled back to the castle. Eight years before, having failed to finalize the sale of Shahwan, the discussion soon turned to the possibility of negotiating a lease of Shahwan. An almost magical thing occurred: Mike was able to negotiate a lease for three years of his soul mate, Shahwan. Mike told me, how after two days of beer drinking, with lots of coffee, as the Germans usually do during negotiations, Herr Dieckman entered the kitchen after consultation with his family and stated in his deep German voice: "Shahwan will go to America."

Mike was stunned and just stood there.

He thought, Did that just happen to me? That was Mike's dream to have his soul mate with him, and now it was going to be a reality. Mike made arrangements for his Spanish stallion and Shahwan to be shipped.

Mike accompanied *Zalamero on a 747 freighter from Los Angeles to Amsterdam, where he was then picked up and driven to his new home. He then accompanied Shahwan back to Amsterdam and flew with his beloved stallion back to Los Angeles.

The lease of this amazing stallion gave Mike an opportunity to survive longer financially since his business had begun to fail. After a quarantine, Shahwan returned home to Portland, Oregon. Mike and his wife introduced his new stallion to the Arabian Sport Horse industry. That division among the Arabian world was beginning to become very popular. A bright new star was now available in the United States.

In Germany, because Shahwan's scoring in the 100-day test was so outstanding, he had been given the honor of being qualified to be a Trakehner improvement sire, the coveted Trakehner Elk antlers stamp adorned his German registration papers. Shahwan was introduced to the American Trakehner Association and was accepted as the first Arabian stallion to be recognized as a Trakehner approved sire in the United States.

Mike and his wife introduced and promoted Shahwan to the general sport horse industry of the United States. He was warmly accepted and was invited to be presented to the California Dressage Federation annual convention that only accepted warmbloods and famous dressage horses. That was a tremendous honor.

In the next five years, the Chapman's attracted numerous mares of all breeds, including Arabian horses. Mike and his wife eventually purchased Shahwan fully from the Dieckmans.

But even with the success of their stallion, there was still an elephant in the room. The financial troubles from Mike's previous exploits in the Arabian industry were coming to a head. The business that kept them afloat was failing. They sold their business and focused on breeding their famous stallion. The revenues generated from Shahwan kept the horse operation alive. Mike was then forced to turn to his old talent of driving trucks to make a living to pay for his family. In Germany, Shahwan bred forty plus mares. In America, he bred over a hundred mares. Australia had more than fifteen offspring from him.

Mike and his family purchased a property in Central Oregon. With hope that solvency would soon follow, Mike invested his time and effort in the ranch. It was a beautiful place that they loved. Driving became more and more necessary to provide income for the family. Shahwan would see Mike in between his runs. He would always tell him to have faith and please wait for him.

One day, Mike bade farewell to his beloved stallion for the last time. While driving from Arizona to California, a telephone call from his wife announced the news that their boy was deathly ill. Four hours had passed as the veterinarian worked hard to save his life. An enlarged heart would ultimately force a conclusion that even if they were able to stabilize him, his heart would eventually have killed him.

Being so far away from him, the only way that he could communicate with his soulmate was by phone. As his wife held the portable phone to Shahwan's ear, Mike said farewell to his beloved stallion. "I love you with all my being. I'm so sorry I have forsaken you. We will be together again, I'm sure." Mike assured him of that reality somehow. Mike pulled into a truck stop and just wailed in pain and grief.

James said that Mike told him that the only way that he could console himself was to realize that God created his beloved stallion and had given him as a gift. He thanked God for the time that he spent with him and willingly surrendered him back into his presence. He asked God for peace, which immediately came into his heart. Mike assured James that the grief was tremendous, but he knew that his precious stallion was with him in his soul and his spirit.

"He grieves to this day for his beloved Shahwan," James told Mom. "And Mike's wife ultimately succumbed to the pressures placed upon her. The years of financial stress, the fact that Mike was always on the road and finally the death of Shahwan broke her. Soon after their stallion's demise, Mike's wife filed for divorce and took his son with her. The horses were dispersed. All twenty-five of them. Mike was at peace after his stallion died but was unwilling to accept what his wife was demanding. In defeat, Mike finally conceded and moved into his truck only to see his son once a month and eventually only once a year, literally for the last three years. I haven't seen Mike in three years."

James then told Mom that the word was that Mike was in extreme depression. His whole world was gone, everything that made his life, his family, his passion for horses and finally the passing of his soulmate, Shahwan.

"Mrs. Peters," James said, "Mike's mom and dad wanted me to share this with you so that you could understand why you perceive Mike in his present state of mind. I have really good news though. When I heard of Mike's horses being disbursed, I took it upon myself to find these horses. Through much searching, I have collected ten of his most prized mares as well as five of Shahwan's daughters."

"James, is that true?" Mom asked.

"Yes, ma'am. For the last three years, I'd lost track of Mike, and now that I know that he's okay and where he is, I want to make a proposal to you."

"What's that, James?"

"I own a winery over in the valley. Well, what if we gather Mike up one day without him knowing where he's going under some kind of ruse and take him down to my place."

"Oh, Mr. Reynolds! That would be the neatest thing ever. I can't imagine what Mike would do. I need to tell my son about this. James, my son, Mathew, has been spending time with Mike, and all this time I was wondering where Mike had gained all that knowledge.

"He's passionate about his horses, and it comes from his spirit."

"Oh, thank you so much for sharing this with me. Let's get together later and make arrangements, okay? I need to tell my son right away. Please tell Mrs. Chapman that we have communicated. Thanks much."

"Please be in touch. You have my phone number, Mrs. Peters. Goodbye."

CHAPTER 25

Miya's Forgiveness

The smell of bacon and eggs cooking greeted me. Mom was up quite early, and her exuberance was palpable. I wandered downstairs rubbing my eyes, noticing the obvious difference in my mother. The music was on in the background that contributed to the feeling of excitement. Mom usually didn't have the '50s station on. "Come on Mathew, eat your breakfast. I have some fresh orange juice for you. And some pancakes if you want. What do you think? Your choice of syrup."

"Mom? What's going on? You're weird this morning."

"Ah, nothing son. Just eat your breakfast. I noticed that Mike has been moving around outside. You two need to get together."

"Okay, Mom."

"Miya's waiting for you."

Mom knew that I had some business to take care of with Mike. Not wanting to distract me with the good news, she thought it wise for me to discuss last night's experiences with Miya at the roping arena. I took special care with Miya that morning. Upon opening the door to the barn, Miya was standing outside. Usually, there were a pair of eyes looking over the stall door as she waited for me. This time Miya was a little bit indifferent, even when I came to the stall, Miya looked around and turned away. This was not like Miya. I became concerned. Maybe she wasn't feeling well, but really inside my heart, I knew that the experience last night had affected our relationship. I went outside and sat in my special place like Mike had recommended when we were first developing our relationship. Maybe Miya would eventually talk to me as my friend Shirley last night did, I thought. Taking special care, it was difficult to just sit there without asking for Miya to come up to me. Like Mike told me, horses have special needs. Survival, food, and fun. I knew she was hungry. Since I was the only one who gave her food, maybe she would come up to me and ask me for it. As predicted, Miya turned and walked over to her manger. Since there was nothing there, she turned and looked at me inquisitively. I still ignored her. It was too much for Miya, so she came over and nudged me in the back. That was just too much for me to handle, and I reached over and gave Miya a big scratch and a big hug. Looking into her eyes, I tried what Mike had said so many times, "A picture is worth a thousand words." I asked Miya in my mind to forgive me. Funny thing, the answer was, "Of course I do, now feed me."

I smiled and obliged. What a relief, I thought. I retrieved my brushes and proceeded to groom her. Just then Mike peeked over the stall door and greeted me.

"Well, you two look like you're cozy together."

I said, "Looks can be deceiving because just last night she hated me."

"She hated you?" asked Mike.

"Yes, it's hard for me to admit that I really messed up last night."

"What happened?" said Mike.

"Well, Shirley and I went to the roping arena to go watch the kids with their horses, and all the cowboys rope their cattle. We took our horses. Remember I told you about those boys that teased me about Miya?"

"Yes," said Mike

"Well, they were oddly friendly. They wanted us to go play in the exercise arena. Shirley was there with her horse, Danny. He's a really talented horse. I've been doing really well on Miya with Shirley's help.

So, Shirley and I were in there riding with the boys. Well to make a long story short, one of the boys challenged me to a race. Miya was real slow. I got mad and asked one of the boys if I could use his spurs. I used them on Miya. She got really mad at me and threw me on the ground and ran away all scared. I spent all night last night and this morning just trying to get Miya back in my corner. I should have listened to you and Shirley about using those things."

"Mathew, don't feel so bad because truthfully, I have probably treated my horses in the past worse than those boys treat their horses. When we are young, we do things to follow the group. We want to be accepted by them. When I was just five years old, my brother and I were in the schoolyard when these boys came up to us and started to bully me. My brother came to my rescue and chased them off. I couldn't believe what was happening. I wondered why people were so cruel. I tried to be good and kind. It seems to me that throughout my life, that thought of being good and kind was there in my mind. When I was a bad boy, my conscience would bother me."

"You know, you and I are alike."

"Some people would call that being of kindred spirits. I'm impressed with your maturity at such a young age."

"Yeah, I know because when I did that to Miya, I was just trying to be a big tough kid defending myself from those bullies. I felt horrible right away. Mike, my Dad was a big influence in my life. He and my mom always reminded me to be kind and have courage. I remember that from the time I was able to remember."

"Well, you know Mathew, for me that was totally different. That voice was with me, to be kind, but my parents would tell me that, and I would just go off and do my own thing, even if my mind was telling me to do something different. But the one glimmer of hope was that every time my brother, who was even wilder than me, would do something wrong, I would always question him and tell him he was going too far.

He and the kids he was with would just laugh at me and say, 'Oh, go home to Mom.' I had my first horse who was so talented. She would do anything for me. She would climb a tree if I asked her. I had such a bad temper with so many negative issues, issues that caused me to not see the good in things. I would treat her poorly. I had no idea about being a partner with her. For me it was. 'Do as I say. I'm the boss.' I hope when I see her in heaven, I will experience the same forgiving spirit in her that you have in your Miya. You know, I have owned many horses in my life. I learned by being with them to read their body language. Like I told you about body language, you have to concentrate and sit quietly and learn from what they're telling you. I believe this was the start of my transformation into a true horseman because I learned to communicate the way that horses communicate with each other. I had a stallion that I loved dearly. I treated him poorly by pushing him to be just like the other show horses. I used methods that were not good to produce a partnership, but actually drove my stallion away from me, even though I loved him dearly and I thought he loved me dearly. One day he bit me really hard, and I discovered what I'd been doing wrong. That small voice in my head that was always reminding me to be kind was yelling at me at that time. It wasn't a small voice. It was a scream. It took a long time for me to get back into my stallion's graces again. Mathew, how did you get Miya back into your graces?"

"It was hard, but Miya is just very sensitive and she's very kind. I think her hunger got the best of her. I really think she forgave me last night and this morning she was trying to teach me a lesson. Do horses do that Mike? Teach you a lesson?"

"Really Mathew, horses teach each other in a herd. I think she just taught you like she would've taught her foal, what was right, and what was wrong. I'm glad you shared this with me. I just had a great trip up to Canada. It gave me time to reflect on my life. Someday I will share those memories with you. Like you experienced with Miya, I hurt some people in my life. These people did something to me that I felt hurt me badly. It was just on this trip that I realized that I had to forgive them. I learned that we need to forgive others before we can ask them to forgive us. Like you asked Miya to forgive you. I think you realized that she had already forgiven you before you even asked her to."

Mom couldn't hold back her excitement any longer, so she decided to go out to the barn and treat the boys with some goodies. Some soft drinks and cookies were always welcome on these hot summer mornings. "Hello guys. How's it going in there? I have some goodies for you."

"Thanks, Mom. Miya's a happy girl." I gave Miya a bite of a cookie, and she took a lick of my soft drink.

"Thanks. Hi, Marcia. Mathew and I were just discussing the facts of life as it pertains to our horses."

"That's something really dear to your heart. Isn't it Mike?"

"Yes, Marcia, it surely is. Your son is very intuitive, I've found."

"You know, that's why I wanted to bring Mathew up here to the country to experience nature. When I was a little girl, I lived in the country. I never had a horse, and now I wish I had."

I smiled and gave my mom a hug.

"Mike, are you going to be free anytime soon? I mean, will you have time when you're home for more than two days? Mathew and I want to invite you to go with us to the Valley to visit some friends."

I looked at Mom, surprised.

"Well Marcia, I can adjust my schedule. That would be a nice escape."

Winking at me, Mom agreed. "I think you and Mathew would enjoy the trip."

CHAPTER 26

Marcia's Secret

Summer in Central Oregon was punctuated with intermittent thunderstorms. The little dry lake bed that comprises the community of Alfalfa is surrounded on all four sides by mountains. Early in the afternoons, threatening clouds would form above these mountains and slowly converge onto the little valley. Our family was aware of wildfires that would consume the foothills of Southern California. Dry lightning was always a danger to the tinder-dry forests of the high desert and the Cascades of Central Oregon. From the view of the little ranch, we often watched the aerial forest fire fighting tankers that responded to the intermittent fires that resulted. I often ran out to the barn and enclosed my precious Miya in the barn during these thunderstorms. Spooked by stories of livestock that were struck by lightning, I would not take chances with my girl. This was a big and different world for me.

The climate of the high desert of Oregon was usually quite a bit cooler than that of the Willamette Valley. The Pacific storms often encroached upon the western side of the Cascade Range. The mountains would wring out the storm's moisture. Often residents watched as the storms lapped over the top of the volcanic range to the west, while there were blue skies above their heads. No wonder it was referred to as God's country. Our little Peters clan began to appreciate how blessed we were living in this Shangri-La.

Summer was soon to draw to an end. With school approaching, I was anxious to meet the new kids. I hoped that the friendly nature of folks from the community of Alfalfa would prevail at the high school in Redmond. Living so far out, I would be bused to school daily. That took two hours out of my day. I was busy learning about horsemanship with Mike and little Miya. One early afternoon, Mom brought lunch out to the barn and set up a little table on top of a bale of hay. It was a welcome sight since I had been working all morning cleaning stalls and paddocks.

"That sure looks good, Mom. I'm so hungry. Let me close Miya's door, and I'll be right there."

Mom sat down and prepared the food, eager to share something with me.

"Mathew, do you remember when I asked Mike if he had a couple of days to go with us over to the Valley? Well, I want you to be very discreet about this and not tell Mike okay?"

"Sure, Mom." I again gave that funny look to my mom as I sat down and grabbed a bite of my ham sandwich. "I was wondering what you were talking about that day, Mom."

"I know. I just was busting at the seams. All right. You see Miya standing over there?"

"Yes, Mom, come on. Spit it out."

"I have been in contact with Mike's parents over in the Valley. Have you ever wondered where Mike has gotten all of that knowledge?"

"Yeah, at times I wondered Mom."

"Well, Mike's mom told me about an old friend of Mike's who has known him for years. He told me some things about our neighbor that might help you understand Mike's funny reactions to things sometimes. Many years ago, Mike was a very happy man doing what fulfilled his dreams, breeding Arabian horses."

"Mom, he did tell us that."

"I know he did, but, not just one or two years, but Mike has been doing this for fifty years."

"Fifty years. That's a long time."

"Mike was a very happy man doing that. Circumstances changed for him, though. Three years ago, Mike lost everything. Mike lost his business, his horses, his family, and a prized Arabian stallion. For the last three years, Mike has been a very unhappy man. The thing he lived for was gone. Everything that was important to him. Not only physical things but the important principles he believed in had no value to the world anymore. Well, you see how he comes to life when he's with you and your horse?"

"Yes, Mom, he just lightens up."

"Mike's friend has been worried about him. Mike fell off the radar for a long time. Evidently, he was very depressed and didn't have a lot to live for. Driving was his only thing that helped him survive. Mike's friend, Mr. Reynolds, knew about the horses from Mike's breeding program that he had to disperse. He took it upon himself to go out and find and rescue as many of his horses as possible. Mr. Reynolds has ten of Mike's mares and offspring from his prized stallion, Shahwan, at his ranch over in the Valley."

"What do you mean by prized stallion?"

"Mike considered Shahwan his soulmate."

"You know, I can see how Mike feels because I sometimes think about Miya that way. Mom, I can see that funny look in your eyes. Are you scheming?"

"You know me so well. We have come up with a plan to invite Mike without his knowledge, to come over to Mr. Reynolds's place and surprise him."

"Mom, do you know what that means? I can't imagine not being able to fulfill what I have been dreaming about all my life about horses.

115

And Mike lost everything … He's going to be so excited. Wow, Mom, I can't wait to see the look on his face when he sees his girls over there. Mom, you know that means maybe he has Miya's mom, Countess Majestic? This is just so fantastic". I went over and gave Miya a big hug. "You might be able to see your Mommy again sometime Miya."

"We need to be really careful and plan this, so he doesn't know what we're up to."

"Okay, Mom, but it will be really hard to keep a straight face when I'm talking to Mike from now on. Now I know why you didn't tell me about your plan."

"Well, if you are in on this with me the next time I see Mike, I'll get the ball rolling."

"This is great news. I'm in." I could hardly keep my excitement in as I finished my lunch. My thoughts were no longer about school coming up, but that special rendezvous we had planned for Mike.

CHAPTER 27

A Little White Lie

Hearing Mike's truck in the distance, I jumped on Miya bareback and raced across the street. My chores were done, and being sweaty, I stuck to her rather easily. By this time, I had gotten to be a competent rider. The months of intensive lessons from my friend Shirley, falling off so many times, has been a good motivation to stay mounted. Mike and Shirley had always challenged me to ride bareback to help me with my confidence. Trotting up behind Mike's truck, Miya jumped slightly when the air brakes were applied. I held on as she jumped sideways. Mike saw the whole episode in his mirror. Opening the window, he saw me gather myself and continue my trek toward him. "What's that you have underneath your butt. Is that glue? You guys sure look good together. I saw Miya. She was doing everything she could to keep you on board."

"Really? While you were gone, we went on a big trail ride with Shirley and her family. I jumped across a ravine with my girl. Down by the creek, there's this little bridge that we all rode over. It was kind of scary. But she just stuck right to the middle like she had magnets on her feet. Was her mother like this, Mike?"

"I never really rode Countess very much, but she had a good temperament. She didn't fly off the handle very often, and she was a really good Mommy."

"I wish I could meet her mom someday."

"I know, Mathew. It would be nice for me to see her again, too." I raised my eyebrow and grinned. Remembering I needed to be more discreet, I changed the subject.

Mike, noticing that I was acting different, remarked. "You're happy today. What have you been drinking?"

"Oh, nothing. I'm just excited that you're back. I'm able to ride little Miya over here to see you and that makes me happy."

"I'm happy for you, too. Whatever floats your boat. Or whatever keeps your seat stuck to Miya," joked Mike. "I suppose you want me to come over there and spend time with you guys, right?"

"That would make me happy too, Mike. Oh, and my mom wants to talk to you about our little excursion over to the valley."

"That's perfect timing. I'll go in, get cleaned up, and be over there in a little bit, okay?"

"Okay. I'll be out here riding. See you soon."

Knowing that Mike thought I was a little weird, I rode back over to the house to tell Mom that Mike was home and would be coming over.

"Great, Mathew."

"Mom, I almost spilled the beans over there with Mike."

"Be careful," said Mom. She thought it would be a good opportunity for her to change the water on the lawn. Mom and I did a good job getting that lawn back to normal.

"I say, all you have to do is add water to this soil over here and the grass grows like weeds," mumbled Mom as she was tinkering in the front yard.

Mike approached. Leaning on the fence, he said, "I could use that green thumb over at my place. Just add a little water and hire Mathew to cut it."

"That sounds like a good recipe. Excuse me. Mathew, come on over."

I turned quickly and aimed Miya for the house. Jumping off, I pulled the lead rope from around her neck and let her eat the green grass.

"I'm really impressed the way your son has been getting along on Miya. Reminds me of when I was a kid. I practically lived on my horse. My mom would come out of the house and catch me sleeping on top of my horse as she grazed peacefully under me."

Nodding and motioning to me plopped down on the grass, Mom smiled and changed the subject. "What would you think about this weekend. Would you have two days available?" Mom asked.

"I don't see any problem with that. I have a three-day weekend coming up."

"Well, what I would like to do is treat you and Mathew to an afternoon of sightseeing over there in wine country. I've recently found the western part of the Willamette Valley to be filled with wineries. There is a small-scale train with all the extras over there for Mathew also. If it would work, we will leave Saturday morning early."

"That sounds great, Marcia. It'll be good to get out of that truck for a while." "Now you guys go have fun with Miya. I need to go inside and catch up on some work."

Mom quickly went into the house and called Mr. Reynolds to verify the details. "Hello, James? This is Marcia. Mike was just here, and this weekend will be just fine."

"I'm glad. I have made all the arrangements, and we'll be ready. Oh, by the way, I have invited Mike's parents to be there."

"That will be great; Mike will be excited to see them."

"I hope he takes it well. I so want to surprise him."

"Me too."

"The idea of the winery tour was a great idea, Marcia. By the way, the winery I own would be perfect. I have taken that one step further with an idea of my own that will surprise even you. This idea comes out of one of Mike's favorite books. I'll call you and let you know where to come on Friday. I am so excited about this whole thing."

"Okay. Are you going to tell me what you're up too?"

"If we succeed, I think everyone will be delighted."

"All right, you know Mike best."

"Sure do, Marcia. Talk to you on Friday. Bye."

"Bye for now. Thanks, James."

CHAPTER 28

Mike's Big Surprise

With the holiday weekend coming up, Mike arranged to do back to back hay drops at the dairy in Washington. After all, livestock still had to eat. Mike was used to living in his truck. He was behind the wheel day and night, sleeping when the regulations called for it. He was looking forward to the little holiday with his good friends.

Mom had already been in contact with Mr. Reynolds to finalize the plans for the get-together. Mike's parents would be there, and it was assured that it would be a good time had for all. I was going to bring my camera just in case I saw Countess Majestic.

"Now Mathew, are you sure Shirley is going to take care of your girl while you're gone."

"Yes, Mom, it's all arranged."

Saturday morning arrived quickly. Mike offered the use of his crew cab for the journey over to the Valley. There was plenty of conversation on the way over. Mike was acting as tour guide for us newcomers to Oregon. The trip over the mountains included the Santiam Pass, the picturesque view of the Cascade volcanic range, the three sisters and Mount Bachelor off to the south, and Mount Jefferson with Mount Hood in the distance to the north. As is usual in the Northwest, snow and eternal glaciers still clung to the side of these mountains. The sighting of deer and wildlife was plentiful. This time of year, the rutting season forced motorists to take special care. Mike assured us that the big cattle guard on the front of his truck would protect us. It was 120-mile drive over to Salem, which followed the Santiam River part way on its course to the Willamette Valley. The Detroit Lake recreation area with all its vacationers dotted the lake for the three-day weekend. Mike had been over this pass hundreds of times. Except this time, he was the tour guide. I was fascinated by the lava beds that stretched out for miles.

I asked Mike, "I heard kids talking about the volcanoes in the Cascades. If these volcanoes erupt and bury us over there in the valley of Central Oregon—"

Mike interrupted me and laughed and told me not to worry because even if they did blow their top, we wouldn't even know what hit us. But he did assure me that there would be plenty of warning.

Like any kid, I blurted out, "Are we there yet?"

Mom looked back at me, poked me in the arm, and said, "Quit it."

"By the way, Mike," Mom excused herself. "Do you know where Dundee is."

"Sure I do. Is that where we're going?"

"Yes, just off Highway 99."

"Fellow passengers, I've got the map in my head. I know just where we are now. We're taking the scenic back way, through Newberg. I used to work for a breeder of Egyptian Arabians in Newberg. So just sit back and enjoy yourself."

"Thank you," joked Mom. "Do you serve hors d'oeuvres and cocktails on the trip?"

"Sorry, Ma'am, we just stop at McDonald's."

Just to be funny, I said it again. "Are we there yet?" They just ignored me and kept on driving.

James Reynolds knew Mike very well. If he was going to surprise Mike, he needed to be clever. Driving up the driveway of a horse facility, Mike would be alerted right away. Since the ruse of going to wineries was developed between Mom and James. He came up with a plan that was right out of a book that Mike cherished dearly. That book is called *Drinkers of the Wind* by Carl Raswan. It tells about an adventurer who spent his life on a quest for the perfect Arabian horse.

Nearing Newberg, Mike continued his travel log. "We're only about fifteen or twenty miles from Dundee."

"Okay, Mike, it shows you turn left up here on Highway 99."

"Excuse me, Mike, pull in here at this pay phone. I'm going to call my friend to let him know that we're close. Be back in a second."

"Hello James, Yes we're in Newberg. See you in about fifteen? Okay about twenty then. Alright. I'm so excited."

I was in the backseat hardly able to contain myself. Mom opened the door and saw me in the back about to explode.

Glaring at me, then smiling innocently, she said, "We'll be there in about 20 minutes"

"Pretty good timing, Marcia. We're supposed to be there, what at noon?"

"Right up here, there's a fruit stand, turn right, looking good, Mike. Round that right turn. Eleven fifty-five, we'll recommend you for your promptness."

Mike said, "Yes Ma'am. Would you like me to stay in the car?"

We all laughed. Mom and I were trying to contain ourselves with this sloppy humor, knowing what was about to happen. The excitement grew. I was back there just about ready to open the door before we even got there.

"Mike, up here, there's a sign on the left. St. Martin D'Angelo Winery. This is the place."

Mike turned the big dually into the driveway and commented about the beautiful Spanish-style mission motif.

"Yes, Mike. I was told they make good wines here. Pull up to the front of the parking lot next to the Mercedes."

"This must be the place," Mike said.

We all piled out of the big dually.

The door opened to the office and out stepped a well-dressed man wearing a pair of cowboy boots, a nice pair of Wrangler jeans and a Western shirt with a big belt buckle. The belt buckle had a wonderful depiction of three Arabian horse heads. Mike froze when he saw his old friend. Behind Jim were Mike's father and mother, arm-in-arm. The atmosphere was electric. Mike looked embarrassed at first. He reached out, grasped his old friend's hand, and looked into his eyes. They warmly embraced as his parents, Mom, and I looked on happily.

"Let me look at you, my friend," James said. "How's the world been treating you?"

"I'm surviving, but this takes the cake. Mom and Dad and you, Jim."

"Good to hear that, Mike, because you know I've been praying for you," James said.

"I have been out there for a while, haven't I, Jim?"

Mike looked over at Mom and me and proudly introduced his parents.

Jim then spoke up and said, "Everybody come on. I want to show you all something." Jim opened the big ornate carved doors in front of them, revealing a manicured Spanish courtyard with grass and a fountain in the middle with a promenade around the outside, a red tiled roof held up by big stone arches. On each arch, the whole way around, were tied ten absolutely beautiful Arabian horses. Their coats were freshly groomed. Mike looked around, first at Jim, seeking permission, he quickly walked around to inspect the visions in front of him. One by one, he would stop, smile, look around and there, three horses down was a face that he could never forget. Right in front of his eyes was his precious mare, Countess Majestic. The surprised look in his eyes was priceless.

"Jim, I know all these horses … What is this? I never thought … Excuse me Jim, folks."

Hesitating and emotionally moved, Mike turned around and caressed his favorite mare's neck and gazed into her big expressive eyes. His mom and dad stood close behind, caught up in the moment.

"I never thought I would ever see these horses again. This is the greatest thing. I'm just blown away. Jim, those girls? What? How?"

With tears in his eyes, Mike went around and visited his lost family. The Arabian horse never forgets. Each one of Mike's past charges affectionately nuzzled him.

"I don't know what to say, folks. Jim, how did you get these girls?"

"I wasn't going to let these horses become lost, so I went out and did what I could to find them, and I'm still searching."

"This is amazing, and you found my Countess. Mathew, come over here and look at this girl. This is Miya's mom. Do you see what I mean, where Miya gets her looks? Look at those big gentle eyes."

Countess reached down and gently nuzzled my hand to greet me. There was a familiar feeling that was mutual. Excitedly, all the horses were waiting to greet Mike again.

"If it wasn't for Marcia and Mathew, this would not have happened," said Jim.

Mike took everybody around and introduced us to each beloved Arabian mare personally. Looking around contentedly, Mike exclaimed, "All of us souls together here, we're one big happy family." I saw a light in my mentor's eyes again. What a reunion, I thought. I am so blessed to have experienced this moment.

That occasion at the winery was something that I would always remember. That man I admired so much was finally happy again. Mike always told me that God created man and horse to be together. Our promises we made together, will be fulfilled someday. Reassured of those promises, Mike had been resurrected. No longer did he feel the great pain. The joy returned to his life again because of the people that loved him and his precious Arabian mares.

CHAPTER 29

Mike's Unexpected Gift

Remembering that day with Mike so long ago, I was overcome with emotion. I had tears in my eyes as I looked at that beautiful bay colt that was asleep on my lap. Momma hovered contentedly over us. The eyes of this beautiful treasure in front of me met mine, and I remembered a quote Mike shared with me. "She will fill our soul with splendor and consecrate our memories. Let her spirit stand among us forever."

My memories were flooding back again. Soon after the reunion that Mr. Reynolds arranged, Jim informed Mike of a three-year-old filly that was completely wild up in Washington State. "This filly, by *Shahwan GASB, his US registered name, was one of the horses that used to belong to a horsewoman that died three years before. The woman's name was Maria Van Winkle."

"Wait a minute," Mike said to Jim. "That woman was very instrumental in my eventual purchase of Shahwan. When I was promoting Shahwan after his arrival in the US, we sent out hundreds of promotional videos. One person I remember was very impressed by our advertisements. We sent her a video and never heard back. Six months later we received a call from a woman saying she was speaking for an admirer of my stallion. She explained that this friend of hers, Maria, had received the video and was so excited that she had found the horse of her dreams. Unfortunately, the day after she viewed the video, she was shot by a stalker. She was in the hospital, fighting for her life, a paraplegic. During her recovery, Shahwan's video had inspired her. Whenever possible, she would watch the video, over and over again. She told me she would ride again, either on one of Shahwan's sons or Shahwan himself. I was asked to accompany this woman in a special van to see Shahwan in person."

Mike went on to tell us that it had been a warm fall day when they welcomed an excited Maria and her entourage. As they strolled through the barn with Maria, a curious Shahwan came to his door and seemed to be moved by the smiling woman in that rolling contraption. His demeanor had changed as he gingerly greeted his admirer. They had presented Shahwan to Maria in the expansive setting where he would run and play every day. Shahwan displayed himself proudly and magnificently to his awestruck devotee, strutting his stuff, blowing and snorting. He would settle down and return to present himself gently back at her side, lowering his soft muzzle for her to caress. Maria commented, "I feel like we have been eternally connected. I never have been so moved." They agreed with Maria to the extent that it was a mutual belief. Mike and Maria became instant friends united through the timeless bond with Shahwan. Their beloved stallion was the soul that brought them together. He was everything she had imagined from the tape and better.

After a hard-fought recovery, the strength had returned to Maria. She was able to breed two of her mares to Shahwan in the ensuing years. Maria won a sizable lawsuit that enabled her to pursue her dreams of breeding to Shahwan and eventually riding him. She was confined to a wheelchair specially designed for negotiating around barnyards. Maria utilized her master's degree training and would continue to pursue her architectural business. She enthusiastically participated in special training for paralyzed riders with riding Shahwan as her goal. They gladly supported her in this dream. It seemed like Maria had developed a special relationship with them almost beyond time.

There was a promotional stallion presentation at the Arabian Regional Championships sponsored by the *Paraplegic* Riding Program where stallion fees collected were donated to this charity. Maria was able to fulfill her dream of riding her dream horse. Outfitted in *her* finest dressage attire, Maria and Shahwan, with Mike and his wife at the lead and assistance from her able-bodied helpers, rode in front of thousands of teary-eyed onlookers. A special article in the *Inside International Arabian Horse* magazine was devoted to this special event. After the presentation, Shahwan was set free at liberty to wow the audience. Members of the audience were amazed after seeing the stark contrast where the gentle and protective stallion with Maria on his back transformed into a magnificent, breathtaking stallion at liberty.

"I had Shahwan on lease from the Dieckmans in Germany for six years. His lease was soon to be fulfilled when Ewald asked me if I would like to purchase Shahwan outright. 'Of course,' I said. But how would I come up with the funds, I thought. With a lot of prayer, my inspiration was to ask my good friend Maria for help. Maria said she would think about it and get back to me. The answer came enthusiastically the next day with a phone call. Maria had told me she would loan me the money on one condition; she wanted the availability of Shahwan's breedings until he died. She wanted him to stay in America with me. She told me she was not worried about being repaid, 'pay as you can' She'd said. It seemed, the pact we made together from beyond was cemented forever. I will never forget that experience, Jim. It was always my impression that Maria, Shahwan, and I were connected by some mysterious force. Shahwan was my soul mate. Maria felt the same way about Shahwan and our friendship."

Mike told us about a night when, as he was driving in Oklahoma on his way to Texas, Maria had come to him in a dream. She was very disturbed, and Mike was impressed enough to call her the next day. He did not understand the dream fully and what her concern was. When he called, another voice answered the phone saying that Maria had tragically died. The call was short. Mike was shocked and hung up, trying to remember just what Maria had been trying to tell him in the dream. The next night she revisited Mike's dreams. This time it was very clear what her message was. "It was not an accident, please call the sheriff and tell him," she told Mike. Perplexed, Mike called the sheriff and was told that Maria was found in her muddy pasture in her motorized wheelchair which had gotten stuck. Unprepared for the cold, she died of exposure. The explanation he received was that she went out to check on her horses and got stuck while doing so. Mike explained to the sheriff that Maria would have never gone out unprepared without her portable phone and proper clothing. Mike asked if they had done an investigation. The sheriff said that they just found her and decided it was a tragic accident. Mike was amazed they did not do a forensic investigation. "Jim, I knew then that we were surely connected spiritually somehow. My knowledge of her questionable accident would always bother me. I think of her physically whole up in the big pasture in the sky together with Shahwan, riding happily, awaiting our reunion. You know Jim, I feel Shahwan and Maria are my spirit guides, like guardian angels."

Jim explained further. "After the tragic death of Maria, her horses were kept by a trust with a friend on a mountaintop pasture, fed and cared for, but not handled. I heard of this filly from my inquiries into Shahwan's foals. Sight unseen, I purchased her. She was just conceived before Maria's death. I would like to give her to you, Mike, to have as a project. I know that you have not had contact with horses for a few years, but I think this would be good for you."

"I am so appreciative for your consideration. This would be good for me. My new friend Mathew will be happy, I am sure, to help me with her."

"First, we have to go get her out of that big mountain pasture. Do you have a facility to handle her?" asked Jim.

"I have my place in Alfalfa that will accommodate her perfectly, and it is across the street from Mathew and his mother."

Jim asked Mike to arrange a time in his driving schedule when they would be able to retrieve this filly. Mike told Jim that he would bring a rather enthusiastic young man with him.

CHAPTER 30

Shahwanyssa, The Wild One

Rescuing my Majestic Princess and meeting Mike was enough of a change, but the day we found out about that filly in Washington would start me on an adventure that would change my life. My move to the country had made me rather sure of myself. My mother asked me if I was sure I wanted to partake in this project. I answered her affirmatively with confidence. A young man of sixteen, my mom was having a hard time of letting me go. My dad was missed by our little family. And now her little man was about to embark independently.

Jim, Mike, and I departed soon after for Washington. We arranged to gather all the horses into a paddock and separate the horses accordingly. Mike had convinced Jim to take Shahwan's offspring and add to his band. Jim had previously made arrangements with the trust caretaker to aid in dispersing the remaining horses to safe and caring homes. It was nice to have these two old hands together again to assure a secure future for these fine horses.

We took special notice of a striking big bay filly with a white blaze. I just knew that she was the one. She was feminine but strong and sure of herself. That confidence would be soon demonstrated as we struggled to load this unhandled filly into the trailer for her ride home. She was born in that pasture. She was with her mother and the other members of the band since they were moved to the mountain pasture. All she knew was the familiarity and social order of her herd. To avoid stress, we included a familiar mare to join her. Mike assured me that understanding of the social order of horses in their herd and knowing their natural instincts would help us in bringing this fine young filly into our world safely. Our goal would be to keep the experience positive in every way possible.

CHAPTER 31

Sissy, Our Spirited Filly

It was late when we arrived back home to the excited welcome of Mom and Shirley. We had already prepared Mike's place for the new occupants. For the last four years, the ranch had been devoid of horses. The facilities had been tested before, but Mike was assured that it was suitable for our task at hand. The mare Mike brought to accompany and comfort our new project stepped cautiously out of the trailer into the paddock. She turned to guide her young charge. Confidently the filly followed her herd mate into her new surroundings. Feed and water had already been provided by our capable audience. We all remained quietly near as they settled in.

Mom had taken time to educate herself by researching the Arabian horse. Leaning on the fence, she commented, "These girls are great examples of Arabians, Mike. Especially the youngster. It is hard for me to take my eyes off her. She is special in every way."

Mike chimed in, beaming with pride, "Thanks. Now I know where Mathew gets his talent, Marcia. This filly is by my special stallion, Shahwan."

Shirley was impressed with our new Arabian too. "Is that other mare rideable?" she asked.

"If she is, Shirley, are you warming up to an Arab?" asked Mike.

"Quality is evident here, Mr. Chapman."

"Indeed," said Mike. "Her past owner was into dressage horses."

"You know, Mathew, Arab or not, as I get older, dressage is becoming more attractive."

"Maybe we can do this 'dersage thing' together Shirley," said Mathew, looking rather oblivious.

Mike winked at Shirley and laughed. "I can see that happen for both of you. I chose this mare to help with the teaching of our bay filly. I remember that this mare was once Maria's very talented dressage horse. She might be rusty, but I sense she will be brought back easily, with the help of some future accomplished riders. This untouched filly has tremendous aptitude also," Mike said as he glanced over at two dreamy eyed kids. "Besides, our companion mare was chosen for her leadership."

The big bay filly would soon seek the haven of her new guardian. I remember Mike's saying, "Safety, food, then fun. So far so good." Mike and I were looking forward to the fun.

Since I was starting school in a couple of weeks, Mike reassured me that this project would not be rushed. My patience was tested many times as I followed the lead of my mentor. The news of the new filly caught on in my rural community. Another Arab," they would tease. But I just beamed with pride knowing what I did about where my horses came from, and their heritage. I started to agree with Mike that we were old souls and knew each other before somehow, horse and man. I felt proud that I would have such an old and proud breed in my life. The Arabian horse.

Since this filly was the first of Shahwan's offspring I had met, Mike explained to me why his stallion had been so precious to him. Shahwan had become famous in Germany. The finest Arabian stallion Germany had ever produced.

After he imported Shahwan to the States, Mike presented Shahwan in many venues across the United States. Mike showed me one letter he had received. It read: "It's nice to find you, Mike and Shahwan. I was at a show in Salem, Oregon many years ago. It was a long, hot day, and I was about to head home when you insisted I stop by your stalls to see your new horse. Okay, I said. I'm tired but probably won't be at the show tomorrow, so I'll take the time. WHEW!!! You brought him out, not show groomed, thankfully. I just stood back with my mouth hanging open. When you said I could pet him, this kind, gentle soul turned to me with a look that said. "It's okay!" I laid my hand on his neck and was moved to tears. No horse had ever moved me like Shahwan I just had to wrap my arms around his neck and bury my face in his mane. The very sight of him left me unable to speak. From that moment on, I was a die-hard Shahwan fan ... and will always be." Signed: Barbara A. Bowman. Bandon, Oregon.

Mike said that he would just stand Shahwan out in the open at horse shows and let the people notice him. Instantly, people would gather around. Everywhere that stallion would go, he would attract a crowd. Shahwan and Mike would do liberty together in front of big crowds. People would walk by the stalls and see Shahwan standing in the ready room untied, without a halter, while Mike would groom him with the door open. They were amazed at how gentle and well-mannered he was. "Is that a stallion?" They would ask in amazement. When Mike would breed Shahwan, it was in a controlled and polite manner. Shahwan was known for these traits, which he would pass on to his progeny. He was looking forward to a son that would take on his mantle and continue his dynasty.

I wondered if this seemingly wild filly would have her father's temperament traits passed down that would make the taming of this magnificent creature possible. This filly had a short head with ears that tipped inward at the ends. Her big eyes seemed to bulge from her head as she investigated things. Her head had a deep dish to her profile that accentuated her lovely sloping face down to her wide nostrils and a muzzle that would fit into a teacup. A dark bay color with white socks on her right fore and hind feet. She was well cared for nutritionally by her caretakers. Her physique was strong. She had plenty of miles up on that hill for the past three years. Her powerful arching neck came out of her sloping shoulder perfectly. Her back and loin were short and strong blending into an athletic croup like her father. Long, correct legs with square knees with hocks that moved without interference. Her feet were round and well-shaped. Mike said that she had at least four more years to grow. He would describe her as a flat chested teenager that had not been pushed like many other show horses of the day. This would lead to strong joints and allow her to live up to her full potential.

Owing to her instinct to protect herself, she followed the lead of her companion with whom she felt secure. But, even though she was young, she showed us that she had leadership and strength of character and would often be a haven for her older counterpart.

Mike had a nice facility to handle this filly across the street. He dusted off his tack in that big tack room that had come in so handy in times past. Now to put it back to work.

Mike set out a course of action with our approach to bringing this girl into our world safely and positively. Mike would emphasize that all her experiences would have to be positive. Mike named her Shahwanyssa, but we nicknamed her Sissy. Her companion had previously been named Kashahrah. Kash, as we had called her, had vast experience in her relationships with humans from her past with Maria and was a good influence on Sissy because of this.

The plan was to let the horses have free rein to experience their new environment. We would allow the horses to see us without fear. Mike and I would spend time just sitting in the paddock with them. My mother was very open to freeing up my time for this. Between school work and all my activities, I was anxious to get home to see my Miya and spend time with Mike and Sissy. Mike would go on his trucking runs regularly. He told me that coming home to his horses was the highlight of his days. "The life is back in me," said Mike, "for the first time in years."

As we would sit in the paddock observing, the horses would glance over at us, and we would ignore them. We would let them come to us to check us out. The horse is a prey animal, and we are the predator. They have an instinct to survive. We would not give them any reason to fulfill their expectations. We would change their perception of who we are by our actions. We were important to them in their nutritional needs of food and water and a safe habitat. Even though Kashahrah had not been handled much in those two plus years, we would use her experience to our advantage.

I was over at Mike's house every day. I would often ride Miya over to give the girls in the paddock someone else to relate to. I would put my girl beside them in another paddock. It became my chore to also care for the girls across the street. As Kash was more open to us, she would make a move to come over to us and investigate. Sissy would soon follow. When it was my task to feed the mares, they both waited for us at the fence for their feed. Slowly, Sissy was starting to come around and trust that we were not a danger. She would not let us touch her yet. Mike's mantra, that first comes safety, food, and then fun was ringing true in this case.

Mike told me about the necessity of establishing trust and respect equally. We would become, in essence, the alpha mare. An alpha in the horse herd would not necessarily be the best physical specimen nor the largest or fastest. It is the one who in some way radiates inner strength, an intangible collection of qualities that includes confidence, experience, courage, magnetism, and willpower. With the objective being to become the lead horse and in this case an alpha, we have to develop signals or body language that would be clearly understood. In the herd, the horse needs to be given boundaries. In the wild, the horse learns social behavior and rules from other horses which our two girls have had two plus years to learn from their large herd. We are now taking over this responsibility. We are only continuing this process when we take over.

Our rules must be simple, precise, and coherent. We want to start with a secure life for our charges. This life is less stressed than the horses in the wild which are responsible for themselves. We don't want a new form of stress by becoming the enforcer. We want to take on the role of the decider. Not the one who imposes his will and dominates the horse. These rules vary for each horse, Mike emphasized. I learned that lesson perfectly when I launched into my little Miya at the showgrounds. Mike had my complete attention at that point. Mike also stressed that the role of a leader is to protect. A horse seeks protection above all else. He will seek out that protector, or he will become a protector himself. They always seek someone to whom they can turn to in a strange or threatening situation. A horse seeks freedom from stress above all else; sugar lumps and carrots are not a sufficient substitute. If we provide this feeling of security, he will freely give himself to us. We become their haven. As for respect, we must always be willing to learn from the horse. Mike said that we can use words and tones of voice, but the horse cannot. In this case using enforcement to establish our will with the horse cannot replace the learning of their language. In the next two years, Mike would take me through the steps required to help me gain confidence as we both learned from our big growing filly.

CHAPTER 32

Fighting Our Nature

The seasons come and go in Central Oregon. It was a big contrast to Southern California. Fall brought the winds that dried and blew the leaves off the trees giving me plenty of work to clear them. Winters would bring snow and cold intermittently. The lack of humidity allowed for outdoor living to be more comfortably when it was cold. I often found myself outside in near zero temperatures without bundling up. But when the winds came, I soon learned to layer my clothing. We would see the snow that was in the field blow into drifts. Spring would come with signs of green grass starting to sprout. Snow flurries often lingered into June at our elevation. But when summer came, I was out with my horses. Mom always had enough work around the ranch to keep me busy. I had to work off the extra cash she had put into the purchase of our Miya.

Mike continued to drive, delivering hay to his regular customers. He entrusted me with his chores while he was gone. I happily obliged so I could spend more time with those two new horses. Visits from the veterinarian and my biology classes at school had awakened in me a curiosity about all living things. I asked my vet a lot of questions. One day he asked me if I would be interested in becoming a veterinarian someday. "Really? Me?" I said. Well, that started it. I had my counselor in school guide me in a course of pre-veterinary studies. My mother and Mike were very enthusiastic. I decided to concentrate on horses as my specialty. But, I learned I had to study large and small animals as well. My special friend Shirley started to occupy my time at school and at my house with my horses. Her family became very influential in my life. I learned about the Gospel of Jesus Christ. Mike mentioned that Jesus and his atonement for our sins contributed to ending his depression.

My life was busy enough already with all my activities. Now I had to be educated about that wild filly across the street. Mike asked me to sit with the horses in the paddock and to start approaching Sissy, then walk away from her to show we were not going to eat her. As Mike said, she slowly started to let me get near her and touch her. I would walk away again as I did before. He did not want me to pressure her. One time when I had touched her shoulder, she turned and looked at me instead of turning away. I started to scratch her, and she turned up her lip and made a funny gesture with her mouth. Kash was next to her, and she started to scratch her shoulder. "Wow," I told Mike later. He said that she was starting to accept me into her herd. Soon, Sissy was letting me touch her all over her body. All the while not arousing her instincts. I was starting to learn the subtle language of the horse. Mike was pleased with our progress.

I asked Mike about haltering Sissy. He said he wanted to teach me some things about the way horses react instinctively to our handling. A horse's first desire in life is to survive. Whatever they do is a result of this instinct. He said a horse will react by pulling away when they are restrained, like a rope around their neck, they would pull against the rope to try to flee from you, or push against you when you corner them or fight to get away from you. He called this flight and fight instincts. We, as predators do the opposite. We grab hold of our prey and hold on tight until they stop fighting. In order for us to successfully partner with a horse, we need to unlearn our predator instincts. Horses need to unlearn their instincts in the way they react to us. But, it all depends on us to educate ourselves and our horses in the way we react together.

First, Mike wanted Sissy to trust us. I had already established that with her. We were accepted into their herd. They then can eat in peace and have fun with us in their world as we teach them how to live in our world.

Mike put me through a process that taught a horse to accept the concept of a halter. A halter has a purpose, to restrain a horse and help us control his movement. But, a horse's natural reaction to the restraint is to pull away or fight it. He taught me a way to teach a horse to be restrained without the fight or flight instinct being aroused. First, when I was touching and scratching her, if she reacted to my touch by moving away, I would release any pressure in my touch. When she was in my space, I would start softly pushing against her side and increase the pressure. When she moved away instead of against me, I would instantly release the pressure. This next part was exciting. I would grab her mane, which was long like her fathers, and pull on it softly like it was a rope and increase the pressure until she moved, then instantly release the pressure again. With her mane on both sides of her neck, I grabbed both sides of her mane around her neck and alternated the feel of a rope around her neck and a push like I was pushing her out of my space. Mike noticed I had gotten this far with her and he saw that I had accidentally gone to the next step. Sissy moved her feet toward me when I pulled on her starting softly like I did earlier and instantly releasing the pressure when she stepped over. That was exhilarating to me. She was so smart to learn so fast. Mike reminded me that I had taught her to react differently to my touch. I had not reacted like a predator by instantly holding on tight when she pulled away. I changed my reactions, and she changed hers also. We learned together. With the slightest try from her, I would reward her with the release of the pressure. Soon I was able to touch her face and around her muzzle.

Since time was not an issue here, Mike made it apparent that we would take it slow. He has a principle he goes by that he learned from his mentor: Never use force or become angry. Always be patient and never push too fast or too insistently. And on the other hand, don't allow the horse to become bored. This was a step-by-step approach. Setting up the horse for success with everything he learned and giving him the foundation for the next lesson in his life.

One day while feeding the horses, I was in the paddock with them when Sissy pushed me away from the food as I was feeding her. I told Mike about this, and he taught me another great lesson: respect. He reminded me of the lesson of the alpha mare. Sissy was the Alpha to me when she pushed me away. Kashahrah was being pushed away also by Sissy. "Why?" I asked Mike. "What was happening?" He sat me down and we observed them as they interacted with each other. Sissy would push Kash away, and then Kash would ask to join her again with Sissy obliging. We soon saw them grooming each other contentedly. Sissy was the alpha now, completely. Mike said that I am also being pushed away like Kash was.

"Does Sissy respect you now, Mathew?" said Mike. "Can you move toward her to move her away from you when she is too close?"

"I do that, and she responds with her ears back."

"Okay, it's getting late. Tomorrow we will tackle this issue. I want you to ponder this and come up with an answer for me when we meet again."

I went home and told my mom about this, and she grinned knowingly as I ate my dinner and went off to bed.

My mind was busy as I attempted to drift off to sleep. What Mike asked of me was difficult. I was so nice to Sissy, and she still pinned her ears at me when I asked her to do something. I felt bad in my spirit. I wanted her to be nice to me. After all, I was taking care of her, and I was supposed to get her respect and thanks for all I have done for her, right? I tossed and turned all night thinking about this. Thankfully it was Friday night, and I did not have school the next day. I was up early and got my own breakfast. I quickly went out and took care of my Miya. I looked at her and asked her if she could answer my question for me. She has been so good to me. I just did not understand what was happening. Soon I was knocking on Mike's door.

"Hi, Mathew. It's early, come in and sit down. I'm just getting up myself." Mike beckoned me to have something warm to drink on this cool autumn morning. I accepted with thanks. I started to open my mouth when Mike just said to hold on to that thought until we could join the mares outside after breakfast. I was about to explode, but Mike's calm demeanor helped defuse me. How could he be so calm and collected I thought. From what I had learned about Mike's past, I understood where he was coming from. We went out the back door to hear whinnies coming from the barn. Our horses were eagerly anticipating their morning rations. Mike asked me to go ahead and prepare their feed and to take my time in doing so.

"Okay, now go in with the feed and present the food to them."

I was not looking forward to this because of the reception I'd been getting from Sissy lately.

Mike persisted in his guidance. "Go ahead," he said.

As I got into the gate, Sissy approached me and pulled the flake of hay out from my arms.

Mike said to leave the feed there and come out so that we could discuss what had happened.

"Now, what just happened there?" asked Mike.

"She was really rude and pushy and did not have any manners. If I did something like that at home, my mom would have given me heck."

By that time, I was red in the face. Mike just let me calm down and in a soft voice explained to me the difference of how horses and humans treat each other. "Do you remember what we saw when we watched their behavior last night at feeding time?"

"Yes, I do. Sissy taught Kash to stay away from the food until she let her back to it."

"You are very observant. Now, if you were like Sissy, what would you do to teach her to stay away from the food until you were ready for her to eat?"

"I would do the same thing she did to Kash. I would tell her to respect my space."

"Interesting," Mike said. "Respect your space. How will you do that?"

"Well, first I would go in there and push her around with a stick."

"Now Mathew, consider what her motivation is right now."

"She wants her food, and that is all she is thinking about right now."

"You are half right, but we need to approach this in the right timing. Let's start with her respecting your space. When Sissy was a foal, she had a mother that was her teacher. She learned how to interact socially within the herd, and her mother was her protector. First thing in her mother's mind was to protect her newborn foal from danger, to teach her to survive. If her mother saw her going toward something that was dangerous, she would rush over and head her off and force her to move away from the danger. As precocious foals often are, they venture back over to the danger, not listening to their mother. This time Mom is very insistent in her discipline, and she may use a swift kick or a bite on her butt to motivate her. When the little filly tries it again, she just has to look at her or swish her tail to get the desired response. Have you ever approached your relationship with Missy in the manner that you were her mother or in other words, the alpha?"

"No, I haven't. But I can see your point. My mother doesn't have to use her actions twice to get a response from me, I can see how it works here with these girls."

"These horses desire protection and safety above all else and will gravitate instinctively toward that. Your mother wants the best for you,

Mathew. The alpha or mother mare wants that for their foals. In a loving manner, they dole out their discipline to their young ones. The social order of the herd is established with all members. You noticed that Kash was allowed back to eat eventually and they were seen grooming each other afterward. An alpha will let them back into the protection of the herd because the banished horse is so desirous of safety that they will respond to the directions of the leader willingly. That is an important concept Mathew. As you do the same with Sissy, you must let her back into your graces when she asks you. You need to be firm with her and resolute with strength of mind. Those are the attributes of a leader. But love is equally important. The integrity of our relationship is based on trust and respect. You have established trust with Sissy so far; now she needs to know that she can trust you to protect her.

"We have our horses in our care, and supposedly, we have the knowledge to protect them from harm. It is not in their nature to thrive in our environment without our direction. That is our responsibility to provide protection like the alpha will do for their herd members in the wild. She will gain respect for you that way. What you will experience will be the most gratifying experience you will ever have with your horses. Trust and respect where you and your horse will learn from each other. Would you love for your horse to protect you as well as your horse being desirous of your protection?"

Mike and I sat and watched as our beloved mares munched happily. Mike often said that he was like an Italian mother that was always happy to see her children eat. I laughed and said I always like to eat so that my mother would always be happy. We both laughed. Mike asked me to come over later when the horses had eaten, and their minds would be open to something new. With that, I hurriedly went over to see my Miya and tell her and my Mom all about what I had learned.

After a good lunch, my mother wondered what the rush was all about this morning. She again nodded knowingly as I excitedly told her about my new understanding. Mothers are like that. It has taken me years to understand just why, but I am doing the same thing with my charges in my Sunday School class now. I would just nod knowingly like my mother. I asked her to come over with me this time to see the progress we had made with Sissy. "Of course I will, Mathew."

The wind was starting to come up this crisp fall morning. We bundled up, exited the door, and ran across the street. Mike was waiting outside with the horses doing his daily chores of picking up the manure from the paddocks. We both peeked around the corner not letting Mike know we were there. I noticed that he asked Sissy to move and she did the same thing with him and put her ears back. All Mike had to do is glare at her, and she turned around and faced him with her ears pointed toward him. She would follow his every move with her attention directed toward his way. I also noticed that when she complied with his body language, he would relent and let her relax. He told her, "It's all right now. You did what I asked."

"What a great opportunity we came right at this moment," Mom said.

"Did you see that?" I said. "She would not do that with me."

"I think this will be the time to apply what you learned this morning and now from Mike."

I shared with Mike what I had learned by watching him just now. "It is like magic, but I know now what you are talking about. Is she like that just with you, or will she be like that with me?"

"We will see, Mathew. All horses adjust to their apparent leadership. Now is the time when she has no other desires to distract her, you need to go in there and interact with her. But first, look at me when I talk to you and notice how my energy level increases or decreases."

"Wow, you are intense right now, and I can feel it. Your facial expression didn't change any, but I felt your energy level increase. I was sure glad when you let down that energy level. It was making me nervous."

"Your body language is connected to your energy level. Sissy can feel that like she can feel that fly on her back. You must be aware of your energy level because she is aware of your mind and what your intent is by your body language. I don't want you to wait for her reaction to you like she did before. I want you to go in there with the intent in your mind that she is going to respect your space."

"Okay, here goes." I went in with the girls and did what Mike told me to do. It was amazing the response I got from both of my charges. They both looked at me with their eyes wide open. I moved, and they moved. I was worried, though, that I was too intense, and I let down my energy level, and the horses responded with a big deep breath. I went over to the fence, and Mike just shook his head without me even saying a word.

"Amazing, huh?" He said that they read my body language that I had radiated because of my intent in my thoughts. "Now, go over there with the same understanding and after they move for you like you want them to, give them the reward they deserve for doing so. Notice what a change you will get in their demeanor."

I approached the girls this time with the same intent and got the same reaction. This time, I rewarded them by letting down my energy level. Mike had said, "Pressure is the motivator and release of the pressure is the reward." Sissy let me touch her and give her a good pet.

Sissy followed me all around the paddock. Kash, having experienced this before, just went on with her business. I had not established dominance over Sissy, but she willingly accepted me as her leader.

"It is exhilarating isn't it?" Mike asked.

"For the first time, I know what you mean Mike."

Mike thought it wise to let this sink into me and our charges for now.

"Be mindful of the lesson you had just learned while you are caring for them. Remember: trust and respect."

CHAPTER 33

Shirley's Amazement

My classmates were asking me about our new filly. Shirley was very interested in our progress and wanted to come over to see her. "Soon you will," I said. "I want to go riding with you on Miya while the weather is good this week."

A week had passed, and my relationship with Sissy was becoming stronger. We had learned great lessons from each other. Peace had been established, and my mind was on to the next step. Mike had a good week out delivering his loads of hay. As soon as Mike pulled into the driveway, I was over there again. As usual, I did not allow him to get out of his truck before asking him about when a halter would be put on Sissy.

Mike laughed and said, "Now would be a good time. All of the foundation has been laid to go to this next step. Now let me get cleaned up and settled."

"Okay," I said with a grin. I knew Mike was as excited as I was to get on with our project.

Just then Shirley came riding up on Barney. She was ready for our ride. It was good timing because it gave Mike time to get settled. I quickly went over to get my little Miya ready. She was glad to see me as I was dividing my time between the three girls. I gave her a big hug and thanked her for her understanding. Like Mike had always told me, I looked into her eyes and told her with my thoughts. Her big brown eyes expressed her happiness since she knew what my plans for the day were.

Shirley and I went over to the BLM and rode between the lava flows for a couple of hours. I excitedly shared my experiences of the last two weeks with my best friend.

After our ride in the outskirts of Alfalfa, Shirley and I untacked Miya and Barney and cleaned them up. Of course they went out and rolled. Barney and Miya got along well together, so we let them both go out into the pasture. Mom met us with some sandwiches and sent us on our way.

Mike was waiting for us across the street. The horses had finished eating and were ready, to keep their minds on their business. We were ready too. I had been anticipating this for a long time. We went through the entire process we had given Sissy before we attempted to halter her. She had gotten pretty good at being handled with her mane and being led a few steps with the mane on both sides of her neck. Mike felt we were ready.

Shirley mentioned that all the cowboys did was just lasso them and force the halter on them. "It was simple," she said.

Mike looked at me, and I spoke up with Mike looking on. "Shirley, all the horse would remember would be the negative experience."

"This is really different," said Shirley.

"This is a good opportunity to explain something about forcing a horse into submission. That's not a way to start a relationship with your horse," chimed Mike. "I have explained this to Mathew already, but let me make a simple comparison. A horse wants to survive above all else. When he feels like there are no other alternatives, no way to escape, but to surrender, they submit to you. They only do it to survive the ordeal, and the learning ceases. Every time you ask a horse to do something by force, he will only go so far as complying with your request to escape the pain or to just literally survive. His incentive to learn has been diminished. He becomes a robot of sorts. Shirley, wouldn't you want a horse to desire to do something with you as a partner? Everything we have done so far with this filly has been in a positive manner. We try not to have her experience anything negative. We don't try to motivate her by using pain or discomfort. I am getting into the weeds Shirley, but this is good for both of you to understand because I have not mentioned opposition to Mathew yet. I like to say that I become the decider for the horse who already trusts me to do the right thing for him. That horse will willingly follow me. Horses are quick learners. The opposite occurs if they learn that all they get is grief and pain with my requests for compliance. They will react by opposing my efforts. They are seeking relief and comfort. I ask them to go left, they will go right. If I ask them to move on, they will just stay put. Shirley, you must have experienced an older horse that was on a trail ride with an inexperienced rider who is a weak leader on his back. He would do everything opposite of what the rider was asking of him."

Sissy and Kash were curiously looking over the fence at us. Shirley and I looked on as Mike entered the paddock. We had already introduced Sissy to the rope, touching all around her body to accustom her to its feel. Mike walked toward her, stopped, and turned slightly away from her. They both perked their ears up and turned towards him. They were both drawn to him, and he let them approach. A mutual scratch ensued as he introduced himself into their environment. Mike focused his attention on Sissy. Kash was satisfied, and she ambled away. After a period of communicating and soft touching, Mike continued with the handling of her mane to guide her around softly. She gave in to his request willingly, and he rewarded her with a scratch. I had given her lots of attention by leading her by the mane. The look on her face was different this time as she sensed the object in his hand. Her desire was to learn what that thing was. In Mike's hand was a lead rope that was about six feet long that he had taken from around his waist. She was reassured from past experience that there was no reason to fear. This time Mike reached up and put the lead softly around her neck. Like the mane used before,

Mike introduced the feel of the rope to gently pull her neck around and ask her to give to his pull rather than pull away.

Shirley was in shock. "She lets him do that?'

"Yep," I said. Soon, she was taking a step with the slight use of the rope around her neck formed into a loop. Mike took a step and then rewarded her as before. With trust accomplished, he let her smell the rope near her muzzle. She actually took the rope into her mouth and started to chew on it. Mike, while still handling the loop around her neck, put the rope up over her muzzle softly. She had already been touched on her muzzle and accepted a gentle touch. He would ask her to move her muzzle toward him and ask her to give to that. She had already had a small loop around her neck, but this combined with the rope softly looped around her muzzle would mimic the feel of a halter. Mike would remove the loop and repeat until she was comfortable. This time though, Mike took the rope and twisted it to go around her muzzle forming a makeshift halter. Carefully, he would ask her to take short steps toward him and away from him using this makeshift halter. With eyes reflecting the trust she had in Mike, Sissy would take more steps.

Mike came out of the paddock after the lesson with the big bay filly. He exclaimed how he thought she was so much like her sire Shahwan. "There is so much intelligence in her to enable her to come so far so quickly." We all leaned against the fence gazing at the sight of the two beautiful Arabian horses.

"You know, guys," said Shirley, "I just might learn to like these crazy Arabians."

Mike and I smiled knowingly.

Mike only had weekends to work with his two horses across the street before he was back in the truck. He gave me plenty to do while he was gone. I took care of the girls for him and continued with Sissy's education. I learned a lot from my experience. Mike would guide me through the next phase and check on my progress with Sissy. Those jewels of useful information helped me with my Miya. The winters in Central Oregon were often cold with intermittent snowfalls, often covering the ground for weeks. I would be right out there in the weather working with my charges. I couldn't wait to get home. Mom had to remind me to get my school work done. I was serious about becoming a veterinarian. I was especially interested in equine reproduction. Mike had gone to school for that specialty and had a breeding lab of his own when he was running his Arabian horse breeding operation. He would host mares to be bred to his stallions at his farm. He told me about his experiences with breeding and caring for mares. Mike said that he had bred and foaled out at least a hundred mares and raised just as many foals. I was looking forward to someday having a foal of my own.

I took my mother's suggestions to concentrate on my studies seriously. During my high school years, I would seek out anyone who had horse breeding experience and visit their farms. Not having a father, I really appreciated the example Mike showed me by being a strong and caring individual. Dr. Edmonds, our local horse veterinarian, let me ride with him on his daily routine treating horses and large animals. My neighbor worked for the local radio station in town. He introduced me to the station manager. I ended up working on the FM radio format after school for gas money and to help with the expenses for the horses. My life was busy enough by then. I was also in band, choir, the swimming and diving teams in the summer, and I had 4-H activities and my best friend Shirley. I managed to have enough time for my first love, the horses.

The makeshift halter that Mike had fashioned out of a lead rope was soon replaced by the real thing. Mike had made a rope halter for her. A halter that was built to be strong enough but fine in its construction so as to give the horse an opportunity to feel all the signals that the handler communicates because pressure is exerted into a smaller space. A flat conventional halter makes it more difficult for the handler to get his message across. It was better for the feel of a mosquito than a hammer. Mike emphasized the importance of a soft touch. Rather than an escalation of intensity in the use of our aids to elicit a response, we use a graduated approach where the horse is rewarded when he responds to less and less intensity. We want the horse to become so sensitive to our touch that she will gradually be responding to our mind.

CHAPTER 34

Horse Listener

At sixteen, all my distractions of school, extracurricular activities and my budding interest in the opposite sex would keep me busy. But, that man across the street and those Arabian horses had sparked something in my soul. I felt that I belonged with Arabian horses and there was a familiarity with Mike that I couldn't explain. He was my mentor.

Mike would often explain to me that he believed that we were all together, man and beast, in some sort of pre-existence, created by God for a purpose. We were all sent down to earth. If we found each other during our lives, we might be able to help each other. He told me how he felt about his stallion, Shahwan. He felt that they were soulmates with a special purpose to fulfill. The Arabian horse was especially precious to him. Mike told me that after he came out of his deep depression, he was a new man. Different, because he was not an angry, aggressive man anymore. Life was precious to him. With his acceptance of Christ's atonement, he woke up each morning thanking God for his new life. Things were clearer to him because he had lost all his negative issues.

I remember the stories he told me of what the horses were thinking when he was communicating with them and his awareness of their body language that was heightened because of his change of heart. I knew I wanted to learn from this man. The first time he started to realize he had a gift for communicating with horses in a special way, he was trimming the feet of some horses belonging to an Arabian horse preservationist. They owned six older stallions that they had collected from all over the country and the world. One stallion was very wary of his trimming experience. Mike took special care to understand this older stallion. He said that as he looked into his eyes for that connection, a wave of fear and panic came to him from the stallion's mind. They were all coming in pictures. It affected Mike so much in his spirit that he had to quit and ponder what he had just experienced. He realized in one moment that the stallion had projected a flurry of pictures and strong fear into his unsuspecting mind.

"What a revelation!" he'd told me. "I saw pictures without lengthy consideration and interpretation, but the first impression that came to my mind." He stood there for a while contemplating what had just happened. With empathy and a quiet demeanor, Mike told the stallion in his mind, in pictures, that he understood what was causing his trepidation. There it was again, in pictures, the first impression he felt was relief from the old stallion. After that, Mike had no problem with him. After the intimate communication he had experienced, he realized that a quiet, sensitive approach with nonverbal communication, using pictures, not dismissing first impressions, had calmed a fearful, powerful stallion.

This experience initiated a series of events that would change Mike's life with horses. He already had an innate ability to read the body language of horses. But now, softening and going within and listening was the new frontier. He was already known to be a horse whisperer, but now he realized that the horse whispers in our ears and it is our task to listen. It now had begun to awaken a realization of a deeper, more spiritual mode of equine communication. With this new dimension, Mike embarked on a journey, to become a horse listener.

Mike told me of another experience when he worked for an Arabian Dinner Theater in Florida as assistant to the head trainer. He purposely used his newfound technique to reassure a mare who had been involved in a chariot accident. She had been rehabilitated by another professional and was ready to be inserted back into the performance. The trainer told Mike he was not sure of her success, so Mike said he would talk to her. He introduced himself and asked her what was wrong. She said she was fine with all her training but was worried about why everyone was taking all of these precautions. She was following her instinct to survive. He assured her he was aware of the concerns, that they were just trying to protect her. She said that she did not need all that care because she trusted her trainer. She immediately calmed down and told him she would do just fine. Just before the performance, he told the trainer there was no need to worry. Relieved, the trainer said he had worked so hard to help her succeed. When the horse-drawn chariots were driven past Mike on the way into the ring, the mare looked over at him, as if to say, "Watch this," and proceeded to perform perfectly, much to the relief of all her crew.

Another horse in the same show had to stand in a dark place for forty-five minutes waiting for his part in the show. He felt he was being neglected and not appreciated. Mike reassured him that he was an integral part of the performance, even if his part was only for a minute in the program. He had been grumpy and uncooperative before his conversation with Mike. His countenance changed immediately, and he beamed with pride and confidence. His attitude change resulted in him being the most popular horse in the program.

Mike told me he would do his best to help me improve my communication skills. I felt honored that he would try to impart his knowledge to me. He said the first impression that comes to mind with the pictures is always the right one and to go with it. Stop trying to interpret your first impression. "From little things we achieve great things." In other words, relax and let it happen and stop trying so hard.

CHAPTER 35

Mike's Spirit Guides

I became aware of the colt who was bouncing around the stall, independent of his mother enough to come over to investigate that two-legged creature who was sharing his stall. Today I had special visitors. My Mom and sister had come over to visit the new addition. We all had a mutual love for horses. They were happy to stay for a while so that my sister could get her monthly fix with my horses. Mom had a proud look on her face, a look of contentment. In moving to Oregon, she had made the right investment in changing the lives of all of us kids.

My sister had made a good life for herself. She was a free spirit. She had opened a Birkenstock shoe store in Portland. She and another individual were the first to introduce the shoe to the Northwest. Happy to be close to her family, she visited often.

It was a long day with all the visitors paying their respects. I wished my family goodbye. It was time to put our little colt and proud Momma to bed. A good first-time mother, patiently kept up with her bundle of energy who was just chewing on my shirt and shoe and anything else he could get his mouth onto. The events that led to this colt's birth defy imagination. My memories that had molded my life story keep flooding in, especially …

One day when Mike came rolling into his place with me waiting excitedly, I noticed a change in his demeanor as he opened his door. I was young, but Mike had emphasized how important it was to notice the slightest change in our environment. I think it came from his way with horses. I was absorbing details around me that I would not have noticed before. I asked Mike what was happening, after excusing myself for being nosey. I followed him out to see the horses. We looked out at the white landscape. The horses were quietly dredging the snow aside for that elusive sprout. They looked up as they noticed our gaze with white glistening off their whiskers, uninterested, they resumed their foraging. Looking into the blue sky, quietly he said he was visited by an old friend the night before. I looked at him inquiringly.

"In a dream," he said. "Do you remember when I told you about my old friend Maria, the owner of Sissy and Kash and the dream where she told me about her mysterious death."

"I do."

"After becoming a new person in Christ, it had brought me out of my depression, making me more sensitive to the spirit. You may call it the Holy Ghost along with the spirits of other close friends, including the spirit of horses that were very close to me. I call them spirit guides. Maria let me know she is happy with what is happening with her girls and she and Shahwan are always there in the spirit guiding us. You too, Mathew."

"Wow," I said, "I often think of my Dad and how he is looking down on me and helping me. My sense is that they are guiding us and telling us that there are more good things to come and to not give up on our goals."

"You are right, Mathew. I am driven to bring back the legacy of Shahwan, and he is quietly encouraging me along with Maria every night in my dreams. I also have inspiration that comes from somewhere out there. Like out there in the big blue expanse. I get dramatic, but this is how I feel. This is a beautiful world that God has created for us and his creatures. I feel like it is my calling to share what we have been experiencing with our new charges, Sissy and Kash. There is an alternative to the way a segment of the horse industry has been paralyzed by a lack of knowledge of how to partner with their horses. I think if I could reach out and spread the word to the horsemen of the world, I could make a difference. I have come a long way in contrast with how I first dealt with horses. I have to do a lot of apologizing in the hereafter to the horses that had come up against my strong will." Mike paused. "Thank you for noticing that I needed to vent."

"It is your fault," I said. "All of those talks you have drilled into me have made a dent in this brain of mine."

"I am thankful for you too," said Mike, "I learn a lot from you, also." We just stood there in the brisk cold in deep thought, the white backdrop with two bay horses foraging in front of us.

CHAPTER 36

College Bound

The winter was long with many more episodes spent together with our horses. My schooling was dispersed with all my other interests. I wondered how I could fit all the activities in. I just called it a boy with many interests and a lot of energy to burn off. I rode along with our local vet, Dr. Edmonds, often with my eye on vet school someday. The days were growing longer, and the horses were shedding profusely. Central Oregon winters would drag on into June with a dusting of snow often greeting us when we woke up. The green grass was returning, and I would spend many hours with the horses lounging on the green pastures with them. I was anxious to start introducing Sissy to weight on her back. "She is four years old now and is ready to ride," I continually exclaimed.

"Shirley and the gang at 4-H are egging you on, huh Mathew," Mike said. "Remember patience. We have plenty of time. The result will be amazing, you will see."

Her halter lessons were coming along well with the rope halter that Mike had made for her. I was surprised how well she was doing. Mike taught me to lower her head with a light touch. Sissy seemed to like lowering her head for me as I would offer her blades of green grass. Kash would join us too. Mom had been learning to work with horses. She finally gave in after all my badgering and started joining me when her activities would allow. She had a lot of aptitude. A natural, really. Kash, with her vast experience, helped in two ways. Mom started to learn to ride on Kash. Sissy looked up to Kash when she was unsure, carefully watching every move and later seemingly asking Mike and me to include her. Mike taught me about bringing a horse up in her education slowly by building a foundation. Each lesson would give them the necessary building blocks so that they could progress. He would emphasize, creating in the horse, a natural curiosity and desire to learn the next step.

"Before I get onto her back," Mike said, "we must first teach the horse to do the same things on the ground that we would eventually do on their back." A seamless approach, he would say. I would watch the videos of her sire, Shahwan, with Mike often. It was uncanny how much like her father Sissy was in her attitude and learning ability. She had a beautiful disposition. The approach we used in taming her allowed her trust to grow and brought out the beautiful temperament inside of her. I had to be taught to take things slowly. Changing my natural tendencies to act like a predator felt unnatural at first. Mike reminded me that it was not the horse that had the problem, it was usually the human. We had to become like a horse in every way, to speak their language. Not only to whisper to them but also to listen and read their body language. A horse, similarly, has to learn to read us and not feel any danger. Thus, the trust and respect element. A horse in its natural environment would react in ways opposite of what we desire of it. Horses learned this from their instinct to protect themselves. Since we build trust, the horse will soon learn to alter these habits. Mike taught Mom to use the method of pressure and release to teach the horse. A gradual increase in pressure on their side, asking them to move over with a release in pressure as a reward when they would relent and move away as we had asked. Similarly, a gradual increase in pressure is used when we ask them to move forward with a release the moment they comply. Mike would say that he would instill in the horse's mind that it was more comfortable to give way to the pressure. On the other side of the pressure is a better place.

Mike used Kash to demonstrate these techniques. I would practice on Miya along with Mom, she would patiently give way to me as I fumbled in my learning. Now to try this on Sissy. She had become acquainted with my touch on all parts of her body. She would stand quietly while I would pick up her feet and she soon developed a liking for grooming. She would often try to groom me back. I found it flattering that she would accept me into her world like that. With pressure and release, she learned to move away from me on her forehand, then do the same on her haunches. I taught her to back up, then willingly come back to me. With the pressure from the energy of my body language, she soon needed no touch to do the same exercises. She learned to lead, follow, and to stop and change directions. Soon she was leading from both sides. "Basic ground education," Mike would say.

The weather was getting much better for the footing in the round pen. It was sufficient to allow Sissy playtime with me before we embarked on our lessons. Mike taught me what an alpha mare would do in the wild to move other horses around. Sissy would respond to my movement through play. She and I were learning from each other. Play was important to stimulate her mind. As the weather got better, I would attract attention from the kids in the neighborhood as they rode by. Groups of kids, and adults at times, would gather to see how our so-called wild horses were coming along. Their impressions of those A Rabs, with their exuberance and schizoid reputations, were starting to change. Mike was becoming well-known for his prowess in teaching and training. He was asked to conduct clinics in our 4-H group and other horse clubs. His dream of propagating a change in people's attitudes and their methods in dealing with horses was being fulfilled.

Mike had noticed that Sissy and I had become proficient in our groundwork. Both our liberty and lead work were sufficient, he said, to enter us in the county fair in August in showmanship. Mike said that Miya was coming along well enough that I could enter her into the performance classes. Shirley was really excited because she wanted someone to ride with while she practiced and took lessons. With the odd jobs that I was doing around Mike's place, I was making enough money to take riding lessons along with her. I convinced Shirley to ride Kash. I think I made a believer out of her when she rode my dingy Arabs. She even asked me if she could ride Miya someday. Since she had spent so much time with Mike and me around our horses, I think the intelligence and spirit of the Arabian horse were rubbing off on her. She was asking more questions of Mike about our approach in guiding our horses along. We were spending so much time together, she asked me to the Sadie Hawkins Dance. I shyly said yes since I was starting to notice that she was more than my best friend. My mother was acting as my counselor as she had been since Dad died. She taught me all about how to treat a lady, to protect and respect her, since I was becoming closer to being a man every passing day.

"A lady," I said. "She is my best friend."

Shirley was becoming a fine young woman, and I was fortunate to have such a fine and talented young woman to grow with as best friends. Mike would often comment in a manly way the same sentiment. I would just turn red and change the subject. Shirley is really something, I would think. She asked me to go to church with her now and again. She went to church in a weird way. Three times a day on Sunday. She never would show her horses on Sunday. I thought that was different and it was a good example she was setting. My mother would be sure to emphasize this fact.

Mike was forced to consider making changes to his runs in his truck to accommodate his increased activities with his teaching, training, and clinics. His mood had drastically changed for the better. It didn't hurt him, he would say, to get out of that truck. He and my mother were spending time together. Mom was getting over the grief of losing Dad and was feeling more like herself. The increased activity with her volunteering at school and her participation with the horses was making her happy. I actually started to look at them differently together. Hmm, I would think. He was already like a dad to me.

Sissy was a willing pupil in all she experienced with her new life. She started to look forward to our time together playing and learning. She seemed to adapt to it. I would ride Miya, and Mike would jump on Kash and pony Sissy around. Whenever we would ride Kash, we would try to do it with Sissy in our presence. Mike had a big pasture where Sissy could run and follow happily. Sitting on the fence one day, Sissy was near me, and I put my foot on her back. She accepted the pressure willingly. I leaned over and put my weight lightly over her back, and she just stood there without any trepidation. All the time we spent preparing her for this moment had paid off. Kash gave her a sense of ease and security. Mike always said that in us, we had developed a safe haven where Sissy was concerned. Nonchalantly, we would increase the occurrences where our weight would be felt on her back. One day when Mike had Sissy on a halter and lead, I quietly slipped my leg over her back and laid there hugging her neck. Sissy looked back at me as if to say, "Well, what took you so long?" My heart was beating out of my chest, but she looked at Mike, and he assured her that I was okay and everything was fine. The exhilaration I felt was intense. I felt at one with Sissy. I thought, here I am sitting atop of this powerful creature, and she accepted it. Will this be, as I have read, the start of a coexistence that was pre-ordained, a partnership that had helped to civilize the world?

Mike noticed my visible reaction and sensed what I was feeling. He said, "This is why we place such value on our relationship with our horses and what we must share with the world. Have courage and be kind, Mathew. We have a big task ahead of us."

That summer was a memorable one. I showed my Miya and took Sissy into the ring in showmanship. We did very well, and I got a blue and qualified for the state fair. Both of my horses competed at fair and took away very high marks. My relationship with Shirley grew stronger. She helped me with my preparations for the fair since she had competed in the junior and senior divisions in 4-H for years. Her family was very helpful and hauled our horses over to Salem. I had Shirley jealous at times since the girls were mostly involved in the horse project. I was a minority being a boy. I just remembered what my mom always said, "Just treat her like a lady and respect her and protect her." I look back now and see how Shirley was preparing me for things to come. Very important things.

While we were preparing for the fair, there were opportunities to sit on Sissy and innocently visit with each other and talk while doing so. Sissy accepted and seemed to welcome the attention and partnership. I would take Miya and pony Sissy along with Shirley for miles in the BLM. Since Mike had to balance his time at home with his trucking business, he left the job of exposing Sissy to the world mostly up to me.

I was only seventeen years old. I was so fortunate to have this man as my mentor. He changed my view of the world. Where I am now, I owe in large part to Mike. My friendship and love for Shirley had developed into a strong one. The next year as a senior, trying to balance my time between horses, the radio station and Shirley was a challenge. Sissy's education continued. Mike and I were on her back often. Our guidance using the same philosophy of a step by step approach, building a foundation, was working. She was five years old now and very strong and maturing beautifully. She was an image of her sire Shahwan. The Arabian horse community was taking notice of Shahwanyssa. Mom and Mike were spending more time together. That was nice.

Our senior year was busy. My grade point average was below average. Upon graduation, my plans for going to school were shaky. Shirley had graduated with honors. I had to give time to attend Community College to bring up my GPA that summer to be accepted into Oregon State. Shirley attended our local Community College with me, and we pledged to work to support each other's efforts. Shirley had more scholastic aptitude than me and helped me to sustain high grades. Shirley had plans to attend veterinary school, also. She had interest in ophthalmology, relating to mammals.

We were both accepted into Oregon State. Shirley had relatives living in Corvallis, and I found an apartment. Because having horses while going to school would present a challenge, we decided to keep them at home with our loved ones. They were in good hands with Shirley's parents and Mike. My mom continued to take care of Kash as she and Mike would ride together often. Mom had become quite accomplished at caring for the horses as Mike would often be taken away to his many clinics and teaching engagements. His income increased, and he did not have to drive as often. That was good news for Mike since driving was only a means to an end.

Shirley and I grew stronger in our relationship. I started to attend her church and soon took part in Missionary Lessons. I decided to be baptized as I developed a strong testimony of the truthfulness of the gospel I was taught. Shirley let me know that she had prayed for this to occur from the beginning when she met me. She felt there was something special about me, like she knew me from before. Mike often declared this to me as he had similar feelings. It was not a coincidence that we were brought together, he would often say.

Knowing the challenges that lay ahead of us relating to our aspirations of becoming veterinarians, Shirley and I prayed about the situation. It was mutual when one day I asked Shirley to become my wife. We were married in the Oakland Temple for time and all eternity. The next few years we worked together to achieve our goal. Shirley worked for a veterinarian as an office manager, and I drove, hauling mail from Corvallis to Portland during the weekends. This run gave me an opportunity to study in between my round trips. Mike taught me to drive his truck. Over the years, I obtained my CDL license. We barely saw each other, but our love grew stronger with our absence. Every chance we had, we were over in Central Oregon to visit our family and our precious horses. We never gave them up. Miya was growing older. I hoped to breed her someday and fulfill a hope that Mike had in furthering her bloodline.

One day Shirley peeked in at me and shared with me a pregnancy test which had a nice little plus sign on it. I just about fell over, it was the most exhilarating moment of my life to know that new life between my loved one and myself was happening.

After three years, we were undeterred from our goals. Somehow, we had the resources to manage a now growing family and schooling. As often as we were over to visit the family, I would look over at Mike and Mom and wonder if they would ever consider joining together as an ultimate team.

Oregon State University had a new veterinary program that was a cooperative effort of three Universities. Oregon, Washington, and Idaho. A four-year program that would take a student from Corvallis, Oregon; Pullman, Washington; and Moscow, Idaho. Shirley's interest in ophthalmology would take her to a specialty school later on after her graduation. My interest was in equine reproduction. I wanted to learn all there was to know about the subject and followed the new research. There was much demand being generated in the collection of viable semen from stallions and promising research into the collection of viable embryos and possibly implanting them in surrogate mares. I wanted to be in on that trend. Kansas State University and Colorado State University were the schools of choice for our future in these fields.

Fortunately, we managed to procure scholarships and sponsorships with little use of student loans. We persisted in our efforts. Our first child, Little Josie, came to us healthy and we thanked God for our happiness and prosperity. We had already been through five long years of study. With the help of our advisors, or liaisons and the support of local Veterinarians for the next year and a half, we worked on both of us being accepted to veterinary school. Our liaisons were quite positive about our possibilities but being accepted together would be an issue. We both hoped for the best. Shirley and I applied to Oregon State Tri-State Veterinary School Program, Colorado State, and Kansas State. Our thinking was to give it a go and decide later between these three institutions if we were accepted of course. The wait for a response was excruciating. Our BS was to be wrapped up, and we hoped to know of our approval by midsummer so we could make plans accordingly.

Josie was two and already had an interest in horses. "Horsie this and horsie that." That sounds familiar, I would think. Mom and Mike were happy to see her grow with our visits to the homestead. They were dating and had become close, but still did not make it a team effort. My sister, who would come over from Portland, was becoming a fixture at our family events. She took an immediate liking to her niece. I made it a priority to visit her and take Josie down those stairs to the quaint little Birkenstock store in downtown Portland where she pedaled those weird shoes.

We did not have to wait long for our answer. We were accepted into the program in Colorado. The letter made it clear that they had never had a husband and wife apply together and made an exception to this because of our referrals that had come highly from many sources. Those references assured them of our team effort and commitment. The other colleges were acceptable also but recommended we later do our specialty work at their institutions. They cautioned us because of the extent of the moves we would have to make in the Oregon program. We were impressed with Colorado State since they had both of our programs of interest. We wrote each of them and thanked them for their consideration and let them know we would be attending as our program progressed.

We decided to break the news to Mom and Mike when we were over visiting the family. Mike's father had passed away two years before, and we included his mother in our plans and invited her to the gathering. We were excited with the anticipation, but we were not quite aware of what lay ahead. Our little family had withstood everything up till now. But a move to Colorado was ahead. The climate there was similar to Central Oregon's. The distance was a little daunting. We were confident of our success. We gathered up Josie and headed over the mountain to share the news.

I was excitedly looking forward to seeing Miya and Sissy. Seeing Sissy grown into an absolutely beautiful mare was breathtaking. She was nine years old now. My Miya was getting up there also at fourteen. Kash was taking good care of the herd, I was told. At her advanced age of nineteen, she was the matriarch. Shirley was the oldest in her family and had younger brothers that took over the care of her horses. Charlie, the youngest was happy to have Barney in his care, and Shirley gladly handed him over to him. The Anderson family had a tradition with horses and would carry it on with the siblings.

CHAPTER 37

Change on the Horizon

We rumbled up to the old farmhouse that had seen the start of this adventure seven years before. Mom was waiting, and as she opened the door, a wafting aroma of warm baking food drifted out to greet us as well as Jake, my trusted dog. Mom, said that Mike would be over momentarily, he was over taking care of the horses. Miya was moved to Mike's place because the facilities were more substantial. Mike had taken in a hired hand from Mexico named Rhiggoberto.

While Mike had his downtime, Rhiggo joined the military for four years. He was called again to Mike's side. It was his day off. He was amazing and cared for the horses like they were his own. He was the oldest of seven children from a town called Ajutla in the state of Guadalajara. He had started to work for Mike sixteen years ago. At home, he had one child a year for ten years straight and was steadily becoming the richest man from his town as he sent home his wages. His goal was to retire when he had ten children. His parents helped care for the kids along with his loyal wife while he was working here in the United States. He had been one of the fortunate Mexican workers who was given US citizenship for his military service.

Josie popped out of the truck and was instantly knocked over by an enthusiastic Jake. Josie just laughed because she adored that Australian Shepherd. The sun was low on the western horizon framed by a still snowcapped Cascade Range with the extinct volcanoes rising majestically. The planned event with Shirley's large family, who would be arriving in the big Suburban, and Mike, arriving soon after that, was stamped into my memory. We were together again as we always had been right from the beginning. This is how families were meant to be: together. Mike greeted me with a big hug, and Josie jumped into his arms. "Grandpa," she blurted out.

Mike laughed and accepted his calling. He excused himself and went over to the car to assist his ninety-eight-year-old mother who was awaiting all the excitement to settle before she ventured out. "Hello, Mom," he said, "I sure wish Dad could have been here."

"He is here in the spirit, son," she whispered to him as she gave him a big kiss. Hand in hand with his mother, Mike assured me that the horses were happy and healthy, and were, he was sure, anxious to see me. But first, here we all are. To see Mike happy again warmed my soul. He had been in contact with his son from time to time and had been able to visit him in South Carolina on extended trips with his clinic schedule. Driving had become relegated to a local man who took his place while he was gone.

With the family gathered and the main course consumed, I called the group together for the big announcement. The controlled chaos of the large gathering began to subside long enough for me to get their attention. Mike, Mom, and Shirley's parents looked on with anticipation. Shirley and I stood up together. We looked at each other, barely able to keep it in with Mike begging us to get on with it. "Shirley and I have been accepted to veterinary school."

"Where?" little Charlie yelled.

"Colorado State University at Fort Collins, Colorado, and both of us will be there together."

"Where is that, sis?" asked Charlie.

"Close enough for us to come visit," she assured her little brother. Shirley's family rushed up to congratulate her as Mike, Grandma, and Mom, close by, stood there with big smiles on their faces.

"I knew you two could do it. I am so proud of you," Mom and Mike both replied as they hugged us with excitement.

"I took my training in equine reproduction with the faculty at that University," said Mike. "Good choice."

I answered with a quiver in my voice. "I knew you would approve. Thank you for having faith in me and helping me with everything. You know, I am doing my best to share the message with the youth now that I am a 4-H leader over in Corvallis in the horse project. That is the only exposure I am sure to keep involved with."

"You know, I was thinking you were going to tell us that you were expecting."

"That will happen again," I assured Mike as Mom looked at Shirley and winked at her. The celebration commenced with the serving of the long-awaited dessert.

The sun arose with my daughter jumping on both of us asking when we were going over to see the horsies. There was a crisp feeling in the air as we heard the irrigation in the surrounding fields. Rhiggoberto was out in Mike's field early to change the irrigation. The June mornings would often greet Alfalfa residents at 3500 feet with a frozen landscape as the irrigation water would freeze giving the landscape a sparkling vista with an eerie quiet where all you could hear was the click, click, click of the sprinklers. The horses were grazing comfortably. The volcanic soil would bloom with an application of fertilizer and water. Soon, the fields would thaw exposing the quickly growing hay crops that made this community of Alfalfa so prosperous.

Breakfast, a staple where my mother had made it a tradition to wake me up with the bacon and pancakes cooking had not changed. It was heavenly. The music was classical with the pastoral symphony on in the background. My wife stirred with Josie dozing next to her. As she arose, Josie looked up and said, "Horsie now."

That's our little girl, I thought as we snuggled before bounding downstairs to our feast. I looked at the table, and there was Mike and his mother. They had been invited to come over early to help prepare the meal. He had added his favorite, sausage and gravy with biscuits that he prepared himself. Grandma readily accepted little Josie on her lap as she was given a well-deserved rest from the task of caring for her charges. We all sat down to express our thanks to God for all the blessings in our lives.

"Dig in," Mike declared, and we all obliged.

With breakfast eagerly consumed, the family rose to clean up when Mom asked me and Shirley to join her in the living room. Mike and Grandma gave a knowing glance. With Josie in hand, they left this threesome to leave the room and proceeded to clean up.

"Mathew, Shirley, have a seat. I have been thinking about your move to Colorado. Have you thought about how you were going to take care of Josie during your training at vet school? You are both going to be very busy and away from her for long periods of time."

Shirley and I spoke up almost at the same time. "We have already thought of that, Mom. We were going to utilize daycare and see if there will be someone in church who can help us."

"Wait, Mathew," said Mom. "I have been thinking seriously about this, and you will need help. I have decided that I will move with you to Colorado, if you would have me. I can rent out the farm. You and Josie are very important to me, and you will need help with many things. And besides, I am going to miss you terribly. There might be more little ones to come I am sure." Shirley looked at her then me and smiled.

"I don't have anything tying me down here. I spoke to Mike, and he supports this and agrees with me."

"Mom, we have been meaning to bring this up to you, but it is even better that you have come up with this idea yourself. It is important to us to keep the family close, and we would have missed you, too."

"I am so proud of you both, and I want you two to succeed. I wanted to let you know that I have spoken to Shirley's parents and they thought it would be good if I brought this up to you. They support my decision."

Just then, Mom called out to Mike and Grandma and asked them to join us. They peeked around the corner. They had been listening intently, and not a plate was touched.

"Mike, it is decided. I am going to Colorado with the kids."

Mike and Grandma acted surprised and sat down as Josie jumped into my lap.

"I am so busy with trucking, teaching, and my clinics that this would be a good plan. Your mom will be in good hands."

Mom looked at Mike and reached over and gave his hand a squeeze.

"I sure appreciate what you have done for us, Mike. I am going to miss you."

"Ah, come on everybody. Colorado is close by. Now, let's get that kitchen cleaned up," Mike said sheepishly. We all laughed.

CHAPTER 38

An Offer Mike Can't Refuse

The next three years would see my mother joining us after the farm was successfully rented out. Mike would visit as often as possible. Josie was growing fast, and she was already four. As predicted, we were so busy that having Mom there with us was wonderful. At church, Mom was attending and volunteered with Primary. She had expressed interest in the church but needed time to see what it was all about. We were raised Catholic with me going to Catholic School for the first seven years. Mom said that Josie needed her there. We thought it was a great excuse, and we thanked God for us all being together.

Shirley and I, with Mom's help, navigated through our Veterinary schooling with graduation looming. Shirley made arrangements to further her specialty in ophthalmology, and I specialized my time in Colorado with their equine reproduction program. Mom was Josie's best grandma ever.

I got a call from Mike one day in the spring. He told me that his old friend Walter from Germany, who was a chief purser for Lufthansa Airlines, had flown into Seattle with his crew on a 747-300. He told Mike that he had an old friend on the flight with him. Many years before, he had made his acquaintance over in Egypt while he had pursued his quest for the Arabian horse. Dr. Rhaman Marsufi, an antiquities commissioner, was an Arabian horse breeder in Egypt. Walter had shared stories about his stallion Said, the sire of Shahwan. Walter had gushed about

Shahwan's exploits and his fame in Germany as well as in the United States and Australia. It was coincidental that they would end up on this flight together. Walter made time to spend with his old friend while on the flight. The subject of Shahwan came up again. Mike and Walter had remained in touch after Shahwan's death ten years before and had been sharing stories and descriptions of all of Shahwan's get. Knowing that he would be so close to Mike over in Central Oregon, Walter made it a point to visit during his three-day layover and invited Dr. Marsufi to join him. Rhaman, having time in his schedule, enthusiastically accepted his invitation. Walter had told Dr. Marsufi about Mr. Reynolds collection of Shahwan's daughters. He was told about Mike's mare Shahwanyssa. Mike told me that they had planned to visit with Mr. Reynolds and asked if they could go over and see Sissy. It had been so long since he had seen Walter and his wife, Margit. Margit, a long-time flight attendant, would accompany Walter on all his flights as his crew chief.

Mike sounded ecstatic as he exclaimed to me what had transpired on their visit. The horses at Mr. Reynolds' farm had the visitors transfixed. As Walter had described his memories of Shahwan's offspring beforehand to Dr. Marsufi, their expectations of the horse's beauty and quality had been surpassed. Jim Reynolds had many foals represented. Jim had made sure that his breeding program remained as close to Mike's as possible. It was not hard because he had very similar tastes and aspirations for the breed's future.

Mike told me the entourage moved their sights to Central Oregon and that Shahwan's daughter was awaiting their visit. Rhiggo had prepared the two bay mares exquisitely for their visitors. Their coats were well on their way to being shed out. The cold nights of Central Oregon still held their grip. Mike assured Rhiggo that his friends were very accustomed to seeing the horse in its natural state. The mares' natural beauty and the healthful luster just accentuated their presence. Mike's crew cab entered the driveway as Rhiggo's eager anticipation in meeting Walter again was showing. Mike had shared with him countless hours of stories of his friendship with Walter. Rhiggo had met Walter before in Portland. He was especially excited about meeting Dr. Marsufi. Introductions aside, their jaws seemed to drop when Rhiggo brought out the two girls. Shahwanyssa had matured and represented her sire to the extreme. The Egyptian visitor had tears in his eyes and was emotionally moved by her presence. Kashahra was in her old age, holding up well. Mike told them that her elegance, extreme Arabian type, and quiet demeanor showed through attesting to her Egyptian bloodlines that Maria had bred. Walter, as well as his wife, were moved noticeably. Dr. Marsufi had nodded his approval. As they gazed into the large expressive eyes of the Arabian mares whose heritage had descended from the deserts of the fertile crescent, the travelers could not resist caressing the objects of their affection. Mike, excited, called me with noticeable tiredness in his voice, with his emotions obviously showing, bade me good night, as he would call me later with more news.

That Sunday after church, I had noticed my message machine light was blinking. Mike had been leaving messages and said he needed to speak with me. Shirley stayed close as I dialed the phone.

The voice on the other line came on interspersed with boisterous conversation in the background. "Hello," a voice in a German accent answered. "Chapman residence, this is Margit. Quiet down everyone, I can't hear," she called out.

"This is Mathew," I said.

"Oh Mathew! Mike has been wanting to talk to you. So happy you called. I will get him."

Mike picked up the phone. "Hello, Mathew. Let me go to another room and close the door. It has been absolutely raucous here, Mathew. Walter and our Egyptian friend have been visiting for the last two days. We have always had so much to catch up on, and this has been an especially joyful occasion. Walter and Rhaman have been sharing their stories with German and Egyptian gusto. The beer and food are being copiously consumed. You know Mathew, I don't smoke or drink, but when Walter visits, I allow this to happen for our European friends. The smoke has been billowing, and the emotions have been high. Walter had not seen Shahwan offspring since his last visit fifteen years ago. He and Dr. Marsufi are as passionate about the Arabian horse as I am. I remember years ago when Walter first told me about Shahwan. That colt that was born with Walter exclaiming prophetically that 'this is the best Arabian colt that Germany has ever produced.' You know Mathew, Shahwan exceeded Walter's expectations and achieved his notoriety. I was blessed to be part of his life over here in the US. Dr. Marsufi accompanied Walter here with his expectations resultant from the glowing descriptions over the years from Walter of Shahwan and his offspring. Walter told me that he and Dr. Marsufi were so impressed by the Shahwan kids they have seen. Sissy absolutely knocked their socks off. For the last two days, they have been talking to me about Sissy. This is reminiscent of when I spent two days negotiating the lease of Shahwan to the US at the Dieckman's in Germany. Mathew, Dr. Marsufi wants to buy Shahwanyssa."

"Wow, Mike," I said. "Can you let her go?"

"Our little girl has grown up," said Mike, "Since Shahwan died, she is all I have of him except for his frozen semen. Mathew, I have also found that Dr. Marsufi and I are kindred spirits in the way we deal with our horses. Walter and Rhaman were originally attracted to the Arabian horse because of their spirit. They were always meant to be together with us human counterparts, they would exclaim."

"I have come to believe the same," I said. "What are you going to do Mike?"

"Well, I have learned that Dr. Marsufi has a large farm or Stud in Egypt. He has experienced similar consternation about how the industry over in Europe and the Middle East was going with the abusive treatment of the horse in the show ring. With his influence in the breed registries in Europe, he had been a force in educating the breeders of the Arabian horse about the encroachment of the American way of showing and its negative effects. I was instantly attracted to Walter because of his passion. Dr. Marsufi has that same spirit within him."

"It seems like we are all brought together sooner or later because of our love for the Arabian horse. A true love based on their heritage as well as their inner spirit that we are so attracted to."

"You know, I have always thought we were all meant to be brought together. God has blessed us this way. Rhaman said to me that he believed it was God's intent for us to be kind. He said it takes courage to keep true to these beliefs. I instantly knew he was a kindred spirit like Walter."

"I am with you in this; you are kindred also."

"I have been thinking that I will not let Sissy go unless I go with her."

"What, Mike? That means you would have to go with her to Egypt?"

"Why not Mathew? What an experience. I have driven all over the United States. Shahwan's pedigree is mostly Egyptian. What an opportunity to see where his heritage came from. I have given Dr. Marsufi this ultimatum. He is considering this as we speak. Thus, all the boisterous conversation you heard on the line when Margit answered the call. Rhaman has a need for someone like me, he said, over at his Al Aman Stud in the outskirts of Cairo. I reminded him it would be a benefit to have me with him to help spread the word about building a meaningful relationship with our horses. We both agree it is important to blunt the western influences encroaching on the horses over in the Middle East and Europe."

"Cairo is a big city, Mike," I said.

"Yes, it is. Walter, when he is on a lay over in Cairo, makes it a point to visit the stud, which is close to the Cairo Airport. Its desert location was transformed into an oasis, one of Egypt's most impressive and beautiful stud farms, a paradise for a carefully selected herd of Egyptian and Egyptian related horses. I am so blessed to have met such men as Walter and Rhaman. I am really considering going with Sissy, if he purchases her, and working with him."

"What if you just lease her to him? That way you can get her back later." I said.

"That is a great idea. Why didn't I think of that? So much to consider. I have been away from everyone for a long time. I better get back to the fray. I will keep you posted."

I hung up the phone. Shirley had been listening and noticed my excited tone. She was nudging me inquiringly. "Well?" she said. I quickly filled her in on our conversation.

"What a fantastic idea," said Shirley. "I think a lease of Sissy would be a perfect solution. You know how much Mike adores that mare."

"I know. With Mike wanting a Shahwan colt to step in and fulfill his legacy, Sissy fills a void left after Shahwan's untimely death. Mike said he was going to make a proposition to Dr. Marsufi that not only will he lease Sissy to him but also accompany her to Egypt. That is where we left off on the phone."

"Oh, Mathew. I hope he calls back soon with the answer."

"Me too."

Most everything at the Peters household was a family affair. Mom and Josie came into the laundry room and shed their boots and dusty clothes after a morning working with the horses. Josie came over and gave us a hug. Mom saw the look on our faces. "Okay, what's up guys?" she said. "I sense there is something going on here."

"Yes, Mom. Mike just called. He has had a visit from Walter and a very important Arabian horse breeder from Cairo, Egypt. Just when

Mike is doing great with Sissy, this man, Dr. Marsufi, has made an offer to buy her."

"He can't do that with his precious Shahwanyssa."

"I am waiting for Mike to call me back. I suggested he lease her to him. Mike said that he wants to go with her to Egypt. Dr. Marsufi and Mike have found themselves to be kindred spirits. Being in Cairo with Dr. Marsufi will further the goals that both of them want to accomplish with the Arabian breed."

"You know how much Mike has contributed so far to that cause over here with tours, lectures, and clinics about our relationship with horses."

"Wow, Mathew. That would expand his reach to the Middle East and Europe. I need to talk to that man. I have always been drawn to the Middle East and its allure. After all, that is the birthplace of the oldest pure breed of horse in the world, the Arabian. Give me the phone, I need to speak to him right now."

"Okay, Mom. Maybe you can influence him more than I can."

"Yes, we have gotten close to Mike over these last ten years."

I dialed the phone and handed it to Mom.

"Hello," the voice on the other end said, "this is Mike."

"Hi Mike, it's Marcia. Mathew has filled me in on what's happening. What's this I hear about you considering selling your precious Sissy?"

"Well, I just had a long discussion with Walter, and he and I agreed it is best to not sell Sissy."

"You mean—"

"Wait there is more," interrupted Mike. "We have been in deep discussion. When a German and an Egyptian get together, there are strong views involved, mostly for the benefit of the Arabian horse. And, of course, with my welfare considered too. I seemed to get a word in edgewise. Walter and I have decided to offer Dr. Marsufi a lease of Sissy, and I will accompany her."

"Well, what did Dr. Marsufi agree too, Mike?"

"I am so excited, Marcia, and a little apprehensive about everything. You know Egypt is a long way away and a different culture. I have always wanted to see just what the horse breeding tribes have to offer over there."

"You are hinting Mike," said Marcia. "What did he agree too?"

"I am going to Egypt with Shahwanyssa and will work, or might I say, I will contribute to the stud in many ways to benefit everyone. Dr. Marsufi and I are kindred spirits, and we will embark on many projects to benefit the Arabian horse for posterity."

"Wow, Mike. That is a bold undertaking. I know your passion. I know you have considered what you are about to do."

"Yes, Marcia. All three of us here and Margit, agree that this is the best thing for Shahwan and the Arabian horse's future in the Middle East."

CHAPTER 39

A Growing Family

It seems like everything comes in threes. Mike was headed to Egypt with Sissy. All arrangements were made to bring Kashahrah to Colorado. Rhiggo was retiring and returning to Mexico to his wife and ten children. He was the richest man in his hometown of Ajutla, Mexico. He had worked faithfully for Mike for twenty years. I learned a lot from that wonderful man and will always remember him fondly. I plan on visiting him someday.

The most exciting thing was when my wife came to me one morning and announced that we were having another baby. I was floating. I have always wanted many children. We were almost out of school, and our specialty education could be accomplished without our children being neglected. That would come at an opportune time because my mom came to us and said that she and Mike had been talking about serious things before he left for Egypt. Mike said to my mom that he could not see himself being away from her. We were like an oasis in the wilderness for him. Mom felt the same about that mystery man across the street. It was inspirational when we witnessed their growing relationship. Mike, being gone so long driving, would come home and my mom would fuss over him, volunteering to do little things to make his life easier. Mom at first had a hard time when Dad died of cancer, suddenly leaving us in the big city of L.A. and thrust into being a single Mom. She would say, that Mike being at a distance while she worked out her grief was a good thing. But when she witnessed Mike's strong, humble character and tenderness, she said she gravitated toward him. I have to agree, Mike came into my life when I needed him the most. I saw a man come back to life, to stick around and fulfill his destiny where he thought he had no future left but trucking. My father built a foundation in me until he died. Mike introduced me to a world of horses. Not only the body of a horse but to the mind and relationship we could build by understanding their nature. This had awakened in me a deeper understanding of my ability to interact with my brothers and sisters here on earth. The most gratifying of all this is that Mom and Dad were going to church and both had visits with the missionaries.

I saw good things starting to happen. Maybe baptism? They were planning to be married in a couple of years. Their decision was finalized when the announcement of our second child was made. Mom said she would stay long enough to help bring the next child into the family where our schedule would allow her to leave her growing grandchildren. Oh, how much I found that I appreciated her contribution to our family. She planned to join Mike in Egypt when the situation was right. It was eleven years since we rescued my Miya. She was nineteen years old. Protectively, she was carrying my little Josie, who was six years old, out on the trails with all of us. Considering my family, I have always aspired to carry on with the lessons Mike has taught me. A few words of wisdom that Mike has passed on from the masters of horsemanship goes like this, "The horse whispers in our ears, and we become the listener." Mike's goal is to take his philosophy to as many people in the world as possible until he passes. I will do everything to help him accomplish this.

I had been given a precious parcel to protect when he left for Egypt that is important in the preservation of Shahwan's legacy. Mike had entrusted to me the tank of Shahwan's frozen semen, those precious straws that he held so dearly and close to him. His goal was to someday breed a replacement for his soul mate, Shahwan, who died so young.

If not for the progeny of Shahwan, Mike would not have attracted the attention he needed to begin to spread his message worldwide.

Nine years of hard work culminated in my wife and I earning our veterinary medicine degrees. Plans were finalized to place my wife in the specialty of ophthalmology in the mammalian, and me in equine reproduction. She wanted to specialize in large and small animals. Anything with eyeballs she would say jokingly. We had planned to receive our training at the same university in Fort Collins, Colorado, with my wife's first year traveling to scholastic venues. Our second child was due in March of the year we graduated. My mom planned to help us through the first year of our specialty programs until she could leave and join Mike in Egypt.

Many communications from Cairo would ensue. Mike updated us regularly. He shared with us his experience of flying with Sissy on a 747-jumbo jet, dedicated to Dr. Marsufi's horses. "It was like a football field taking off. From the back of the plane up to the pilot's cockpit was a great distance. When the plane arose off the runway, I was looking up at least fifty feet to the front of the plane with the horses gripping to keep traction in their protective compartments, a three-horse aluminum freight container designed like a horse trailer without wheels. It would be lifted and rolled into place and secured down to the floor of the freighter. We, as passengers, had our own row of seats where we could join the horses as needed. I cheated and rode right next to Sissy to comfort her as we rose off the tarmac. Sissy took it like a champ. I am her haven indeed because she held on tight to me. The ride over the Rockies on our way through Canada and over the Arctic was breathtaking. The Rockies had a lot of turbulence, and Sissy would literally bounce off the floor of the container about a foot. When we arrived in Amsterdam to refuel, the ride was quite level, and the little bounce on landing was comfortable. But, we did it all again on our way down to Cairo." Mom was on the phone with Mike regularly. It was a short distance from the airport to

Al Aman, the stud in the oasis. "I have never seen so many cars on the road being shared with horses, donkeys, and camels. The culture here is quite different. The facilities at the stud are fabulous. Dr. Marsufi spares no luxury for the horses. He even gives his guests quite the comfort. I am fortunate to be afforded the same."

The notes and phone calls would continue and became an anticipated part of our life.

Shirley and I have never been a fan of knowing the gender of our children before they were born. On March 5th, a boy of eight pounds seven ounces was born without complication. After many months of singing and reading to that little growing human being inside of my beloved Shirley, we greeted him. Mom was there, and we quickly contacted the other side of the family about the new addition. Little Charlie was really excited because he would have another little cousin to play with when we visited Central Oregon.

My most cherished moment was when I was presented with my little boy to welcome him into our world, to cut his navel and place him in the warm incubator. He started to cry, and as soon as he heard my voice, he stopped and looked right into my eyes acknowledging me. We named him Philip Joseph Peters. We longingly anticipated future spirits from our heavenly Father in the future. Shirley and I imagined that those spirits that we covenanted to be joined with us in the pre-existence were up there just waiting to come down. Every day that I came home to Josie and then to Philip, I would spend quality time with them. Shirley would join me knowing that we were blessed to have family close who cared and loved us. Mike, when he was notified, told us that his brother was named Philip. He was proud that we had named him Philip as his brother died at a young age.

This time in our lives, we were ever thankful for the tender mercies from God. Many challenges were presented to us during these days. I was thankful for my mother's presence helping with little Philip. Josie helped immensely, too. Mom was going to miss her job in Primary at church. She worked in the nursery also, just to be with Philip.

Shirley traveled with her training to different venues exposing her to different species. She even had experience with reptiles. As she always said, my wish came true because anything with eyes I have seen, you get the pun?

My experience with breeding took me into all phases of research that I assisted with. In the back of my mind was that tank of semen from Shahwan. The process of embryo transfer was being contemplated with planned research. Someday, maybe the shipment of semen across vast distances would prevent mares and foals from being shipped by transport over land. Mike would tell me of the days he shipped horse's cross country, which was the only means to breed to stallions at a great distance. I was passionate about what I was learning, and it became a part of my life. Shirley felt the same passion in her field and looked forward to her practice. The realization was ever present of the need to keep God first in our lives. God first, family came second with our devotion to each other, husband and wife, and our children. The challenges were hard, but we dedicated ourselves to preserve our family. Our thoughts often would go toward Mike and his welfare also. We loved our horses and careers and our passion for them. Endeavoring and striving to endure to the end, keeping God above all else was paramount.

Philip was eighteen months old when my dear mother made plans to join her beloved Mike in marriage. I was so proud to think that Mike, who had filled the position of father all that time, would soon be deemed to be so. They chose June for their wedding. All who could attend were invited. It was simple. They would be married on horseback. Miya and Kashahrah did the honors. It was beautiful to see Mike and Mom beaming again.

We were all whisked off to the airport afterward, following an artfully decorated pickup truck. Someone tied shoes to the back and an assortment of other imaginative items. While hugs were being doled out, we were assured of their return someday. It was hard on Josie. Grandma had been able to attend her baptism when she had turned eight a month before. I was proud of Josie. She was more together with her understanding that their separation would be short. It was wonderful to see how our little ones exhibit their faith so strongly. Philip had just started to walk three months beforehand. Mom held him tenderly and kissed his forehead. Philip innocently smiled but began to cry as she handed him to Shirley. I think he sensed the coming separation also. My mother was always the independent sort, but today I saw a twinge break into tears as she hugged her entourage and bade us goodbye. I told Mike to take good care of my mom and come back to us safe.

Mike told me just how proud he was to see how I was turning out. "Take care of my pickup truck, okay?" To this day I will remember what he said to me before he went through the doors to embark on the plane. It would turn out to be somewhat prophetic. "I'll make sure to stay out of trouble." They both laughed as the couple disappeared into the plane.

Shirley and I spent the summer procuring a loan to build our clinic which we decided to build in our hometown of Bend, Oregon. Alfalfa was twenty miles outside of town and would not be practical for our specialty clinics. We chose a location between Bend and Sisters in a little town called Tumalo. There was a demand for our talents that had begun to be present in Central Oregon. I had developed a love for that part of the high desert. The horse industry was booming there, and we hoped to grow into a viable service to the horse community that would enable us to grow our family. Mom's home in Alfalfa and Mike's across the street from our old homestead would be nearby, just thirty miles away. Shirley's family was there also. We had always wanted to return to our roots.

Mike and Mom were blessed with a man who appreciated their contributions. Dr. Marsufi and Al Aman Stud rewarded them handsomely. We were surprised at the time when we thought we would not be able to be successful in getting a loan, that Mom and Dad surprised us with half the funds to build our clinic. The deal Mike made with me was that we would have to take care of his mares when breeding time comes around. Mike's dream to replace his beloved stallion with a son of his was alive in his heart. He would often call me and tell me of the dreams he had of Shahwan, seeing his dear friend Maria riding him. The message in the dream was always communicated to him to keep the faith because there was a spirit waiting to come down and join them. "Mathew, this is a profound dream. I will endeavor to make it happen."

We picked out a site and began to build. Meanwhile, we worked out of Dr. Edmonds office, the vet we had used when we were kids. He was desirous that we take over his practice. The general practice he established would help us while we built our specialties. Dr. Edmonds was one of my mentors while I considered becoming a veterinarian. I would ask him questions incessantly. He was glad to answer all of them however qualified or stupid the questions were. I was hungry for knowledge.

Shirley was faced with a tough case almost right off the bat. One of my friend's prized Arabian mares had an ulcer that would not heal in her eye. After medicating her himself for two months, the friend brought the mare to Shirley to diagnose the problem. One of the local vets had given her some Atropine eye drops. Two days later her eye had worsened and had turned green inside of the eye itself. It was one of Shirley's early challenges. The mare was in intensive care for two weeks with round the clock treatment to stop what was diagnosed as a severe fungal infection inside her eye that had resulted from an inflamed ulceration of her cornea. Experts were consulted, and the result was an inventive treatment that would ultimately heal her eye while only leaving a small cloudy section the size of a pea. It left her eye clear with full vision. The treatment was acclaimed and was written up in the *Journal of Veterinary*

Medicine. I was so proud of my wife. The mare whose vision Shirley had saved went on to live a normal life. My practice was growing with the large concentration of horse breeders in Central Oregon. I also specialized in research of embryo transfer and the freezing of semen and embryos. I started training seminars for breeders to manage their stallions and mares.

Grandma Anderson, Shirley's mom, was glad to fill in as babysitter. Grandpa would bring Uncle Charlie, thirteen, over to play with Josie who was ten. It was great to have family so close in age. All the horses were together again: Miya, Kash, and Barney.

CHAPTER 40

Mike's Unexpected Adventure

Three years had passed. My reproductive facilities were built, and my practice was growing. My wife settled in beside me in the same facility and started making a reputation for herself. We were getting clients with eye issues from all over the Northwest and Shirley was called for consultation on many difficult cases. We had welcomed our third child, a girl we named Marion Jessica Peters. Grandma Anderson was happy about that.

It seemed like all was going great for some time when Mom called us frantically from Cairo to tell us that Mike had not come home from one of his trips into the desert. She had become accustomed to him being gone overnight on occasion, but this time she was getting worried. "Mike has a desire," she said, "to go out in the desert in search of the perfect Arabian horse." She told me he had heard about the horse breeding tribes that Walter had befriended years before and was intent on finding them. His purpose was to recruit their help in his quest. Mike always took Shahwanyssa with him since she was so reliable, strong, and well suited for the environment of the desert. This time he had planned to travel far into the desert by vehicle with a trailer. Once he had driven as far as he could, he would debark and travel the rest of the way on horseback. "Mike is so independent. He goes out there alone, assuring us that he will be all right because he has Sissy there to protect him. He is such an adventurer."

I attempted to calm her fears by reminding her that he knew what he was doing. All the while I was crossing my fingers and getting worried myself.

Four days had gone by when Mom called and said she received a message that Mike had been seen by some Bedouins and they assured her that he was all right and needed no help. "Messages travel quickly in the desert," Mom was told. Relieved, I asked Mom to keep me posted. With this knowledge, Mom settled in with confidence and waited patiently for his return. Two weeks had passed with no contact when Mike came driving up with Sissy and one more horse in the trailer. It was a small filly that was the likeness of a typical desert Arabian horse. Except this filly was delicate with fine strong bones. She was underweight and showing her lack of nutrition, which was evident in the desert horse in this season. The lack of forage for the native tribe's livestock forced them to use other suitable means of nourishment. Figs, camels, and mares milk would suffice in times of need. But this little filly showed her emaciation outright.

"Where have you been?" asked my mom.

Mike proceeded to tell the most astonishing story, which Mom then relayed to me. This is what she told me:

Mike sought the Bedouin tribe that Walter had told him about. Years ago, he had befriended a traditional Arabian horse breeding tribe. This tribe had descended from times of old when competing tribes would battle for supremacy in the breeding game. Arabian horse breeding tribes allowed special rules that were followed quite religiously. Tribes were allowed to steal each other's horses, but they were not allowed to kill and destroy in the process of doing so. The Arabian horse was important to their way of life as was the camel and ass that were always foraging for the precious feed that was seasonal in the desert. Always dependent on rain pools, the Bedouin moved around to these so-called Wadi's where green forage would grow year-round.

The pedigrees of Bedouin horses were passed down through word of mouth. The mare was more precious than the stallion and was considered more noble or *asil* enough to place the mare or *entha* at the top of the written pedigree. The stallion is at the top of the pedigree in western horse societies. Walter had been adopted into one of these tribes, the Ruala in the Wadi Sirhan. They were members of one of the greatest tribes of the desert. They were rich in camels and had larger tents than the other Arabs. They roamed from one end of Arabia to the other. From Aleppo to the Persian Gulf, from the Hejaz to the Euphrates and Tigris. This tribe, a smaller tribe, had paid tribute in times of old to the principal families. Today, in modern times, they wander just as well, but have more modern appliances. They were known to be seasonally pastured close enough for him to find them. He was intent upon finding them. He wore a special bracelet that the tribe had given Walter that denoted his adoptive status. The possession of this bracelet would allow favors Walter said. His passion for the Arabian horse is deeply spiritual, and he had always felt drawn to seek out its foundation. So off he went.

He went as far as he could go, asking the tribesmen along the way for hints of where this tribe would be. He hit the end of the road of where he could take his truck and trailer, so he set out on Sissy with provisions for an excursion just long enough for him to find the tribe as he followed the Bedouin's directions. Sissy was amazing as she traversed the desert landscape. There was no path or road. They steadily wound their way through the wilderness. The soil was red, the plant life was sparse, especially with them being used to the lush oasis of Al Aman. The horizon never changed, but up and down they rode. Touched now and again with a little green, the ground was a sheen of fine gravel for miles. The hollows were graced with small pools, sometimes as large as a lake, but shallow enough to walk through. Now and again they would come upon a carcass that was long left for dead. A rainstorm broke up the miserable dryness, but they soon were dried after a drenching that would revive them. There were no trees in sight.

He was determined to find these tribesmen. He traveled on, following the directions given to him. Camping out under the stars, his Sissy would stay hobbled by his side subsisting only on the morsels he had brought for her. Along the way, he would let her forage for whatever was available. She did not complain. As he continued, he soon found himself lost and running out of provisions. For a day, he proceeded in this condition. To his relief, he soon came upon a group of Bedouins.

The Bedouin's horses became vigilant as they approached. Their big bright eyes scanned the horizon to bring them into their range of vision, their little ears twitched from side to side. Surrounding them, one horse snorted excitedly and pawed the ground next to his mare, but with a few firm strokes of his master's hand, he became quiet. One Bedouin called out to him in the friendliest fashion. "*As-salam alayk* (peace be with you)." He was accustomed to being ignored by the Arabs, but this man greeted him jovially and asked a question he could barely understand. He realized he needed to speak to him in English.

"You are a long way from home my new friend."

"Indeed, I am," Mike answered.

Assessing his mount, the Bedouin said, "You have a fine *entha* under you. It is our custom to appreciate a fine mare and relate it to the fine person that possesses her. She is indeed *asil*, as we say, very noble."

Humbled by his compliment, Mike expressed the fact that he was truly thankful for his honor. "Your English is quite good. Could you please help me?" Mike said, "I am truly in need. As you see I am very low on food and water for myself and my mount. I am also looking for a tribe of the Ruala, in the Wadi Sirhan."

"Oh yes, I can help you. In that direction, you will see green and come upon the Wadi. Follow the opposite of the sunrise. Travel in the early morning and the evening to preserve your strength."

Mike thanked him and proceeded on his way. He was happy to know he was finally headed in the right direction and would be soon able to replenish his supplies. Night would fall without reaching the promised Wadi. Upon waking the next morning, he made good use of the cool of the day to continue his journey. A stark realization hit him that those Bedouins had set him up for failure so they could come and steal his mare and make off with his possessions. Panic had set in when there it was, a glint of green hit his vision. He noticed in the distance, movement that looked like a party of horsemen. He thought he was seeing a mirage. Soon, the horseman reached him, calling out to him saying, "What took you so long? We were expecting you."

He could hardly believe what he was hearing. Here he was almost swallowed by the desert, and now he was being greeted like a VIP. What a sharp contrast as they rode up to the Wadi with the women whistling their traditional warbles. A man of noble stature approached him. He asked that my horse be led close enough for him to touch her forehead. "*Masha'allah*," he said. "*As-salam alayk*. Peace be with you, brother. We have been expecting you. Word travels quickly in the desert. Come near me, my son. I am Sheykh R'Ammeri, and who is this? You haven't told me your horse's name."

"My name is Michael Chapman. This is my special mare, Shahwanyssa. I have come from Al Aman Stud in Cairo. I have come far to find you."

He dismounted and approached the man with weathered features. He looked like an old patriarch. When he spoke, his eyes lit up with a kindly fashion and his smile was wonderfully gentle. He motioned to his underlings to retrieve Mike's belongings and take care of his horse. Mike first hesitated to allow their advance and reached out to stop them. The chief extended his hand to assure him. When he noticed Mike's bracelet, he grasped his wrist. He assured him no harm would be done as he directed his men to be respectful. "I see you have been graced with the seal of our tribe. Who has given you such honor, or have you come upon this by treachery?"

"Walter Heuser, kind sir," Mike said.

Nodding approvingly, the chief replied, "Herr Heuser's reputation precedes him. You will be my guest."

Respectfully, Mike said, "If not for Walter, this mare would not be in our presence. She is from a line of horses that is dear to him, in fact mostly from Egypt. I have been a recipient of his generosity over the years. I share his passion for the Arabian horse. I have come this far to hopefully find an example of the Arabian horse that Walter described as the foundation for what we have all over the world. An example of the beauty and perfection of the Arabian horse."

"You are a dreamer, my son, for the horse of your dreams is only in the eye of the beholder. Come with me and revive yourself. Rest and eat, for we will embark together after you sup with me."

Mike glanced over at Sissy, noticing the concern in her body language. When she saw him, she relaxed and started to partake of the sustenance given her. She was making sure he was all right before she relaxed and took care of her own needs.

"Welcome to the threshold of our sanctuary," the chief said with formality. "In the wilderness, every home is a retreat where the stranger's stay may lengthen into years, where his past is his own. Abraham entertained angels unaware. Since that day the Bedouin says, we look upon the visiting stranger as an envoy of our Lord."

With his new friend, Mike settled down in the comfortable surroundings of his tent and partook of his host's generosity. In the morning, well rested from his journey and his stomach filled, he anxiously checked on his Sissy. When she saw him approach, she moved quickly to the edge of the paddock and whinnied excitedly. She had been groomed by one of the men. He had asked Mike's approval the night before. She gleamed in the morning sun with her dark bay coat and deep dapples. He heard the voice of Sheykh Ammeri behind him say, "She is truly *asil*, Michael. To have such a mare grace our paddocks is an honor."

"I found her father, Shahwan, in Germany because of Walter. His treasure, Said, was his father. We have formed a strong bond over the years. The Arabian horse binds us together. It is an honor sir, to be here with you and such fine horses also," Mike replied.

"This time of the season, our horses survive on very little," the Sheykh reassured Mike. "They are hearty and strong. The horse of the desert has to have these traits. For thousands of years, we have bred these horses to help us survive. Our mares have taken care of our young by providing protection as well as milk. They have taken us into battle and brought us back even at the peril of their own lives. They are our treasure. I see that your treasure has finished with her meal. Come, prepare yourselves, both of you. I will take you to seek out the beauty and perfection of your quest."

With Sissy saddled and ready to go, he could not help but notice the many mares with their foals in the paddocks loafing with the camels. Indeed, their condition was quite in a state of general emaciation by western standards. He had come to expect this in the short time he had been in the Middle East. He was excited with anticipation of the potential of revealing the objects of his quest.

The Sheykh joined him as they gazed out at his prize band of horses. "*Masha'Allah*, Michael. I asked you to join me. For the journey of our minds has to be fulfilled. It is indeed what is in our hearts and souls that withstands the test of time. Our participation with Allah is a gift. Embodied here are many spirits that have chosen freely. Allah has provided for them their habitation in bodies of strength and beauty blended in perfection. Gaze upon them for a moment and savor their creation."

With a gentle slap on his back, he was bade to mount his mare and join the old soul. They were accompanied by two men mounted on camels, who brought provisions for at least three days. Their travels took them to the different tribes. They were greeted at each Wadi and campsite with enthusiasm. Through the poor, shabby, disheveled horses they would be guided. Their pride was immense as they shared with them the labor of centuries of horse breeding. They traversed the countryside with their host presenting them with the best the horse breeding tribes had to offer. For three days, mare families were introduced with their particular contributions noted. It was obvious, he had thought, that these bloodlines were here for him to discover perfection. With this information, he realized that their bloodlines combined so beautifully to produce the horse of his quest. But where was that elusive perfect Arabian horse of his dreams?

Somewhat disappointed, his host left him to his own journey in his mind. Now he tried to comprehend what the old man had said on their return trip while they were in view of his precious band of horses. The ride back to the Wadi Sirhan was quiet for him. He was deep in contemplation. Had he failed to find the horse of his dreams? The horses he discovered had all the characteristics of the oldest purebred breed of horse in the world. Was that horse out there somewhere and he did not discover her? His mind was filled with all the mare families he remembered and the combinations he would use to produce the horse of his dreams. 'But, isn't this what it is all about?' Thought Mike. 'We interact with God and direct the different mare families together to create the perfect Arabian horse?' Still, he was disappointed that he failed in his quest. He would take home with him the lessons learned together with his new friend and horseman, Sheykh Ammeri.

It was late when they arrived at the Wadi after their three-day tour. Their horses were exhibiting their inherited Arabian stamina while bearing their weary charges on their backs. He was proud of Sissy. She had not lost, through her bloodlines, the traits that had carried the Bedouin tribes across thousands of miles on their journey of survival.

With their horses prepared for their rest after the long trip, Sheykh Ammeri joined him as he caressed the second love of his life, Shahwanyssa.

"You and your treasure, Sissy, as I have heard you call her, have a very special relationship. We here in the desert depend on our horses for literally our own survival. A partnership with them is needed. We need them, and they need us. She looks for you as her own," Ammeri said.

"I look for her as an equal," Mike replied. "We have come a long way together in our lives. She was a wild filly just fifteen years ago. I had to earn her trust and respect."

The Sheykh said, "You have accomplished just that my son. Please join me as I walk among my children, as I call my horses."

He hugged his Sissy and joined his friend. Walking with his family, he was in heaven. The foals playfully bounded among them and would periodically break away to greet them. As they mingled, his skillful breeder would call out the mare families similarly as they had done on their journey. With great pride, he stopped to gaze at a particular mare with a filly that was nearing her weaning age.

"Ah, my treasure, Michael. This represents the ultimate combination that Allah has seen fit to bless me with. She has been with me through many years. I am devoted to her. I bathe her with tears of joy every morning. The light of my life, the enriching one. Many generations, I have been permitted to co-create with Allah. This filly is a treasure in her own right. Michael, you have proven to me your worthiness." He reached out his right hand and grasped Mike's arm.

He was deep in the moment when he thought he heard Ammeri say, "She is my gift to you, Michael."

He shook his head and looked up thinking he was hearing things. Ammeri put both of his arms on Mike's shoulders and repeated, "She is my gift to you, Michael. Fear not to take her. She will fill your soul with splendor and consecrate our memories. Let her spirit stand amongst us forever."

Mike looked into his wise, kind old eyes and immediately started to weep. He saw an old familiar soul in those eyes. He thanked God at that moment, for he knew this was meant to be. Trusting in the wisdom of this gentle person, he gratefully accepted his gift. At that moment, he noticed that little filly chewing on his shirt sleeve as if to say, *I am yours now*. Her mother was *asil*. He now knew the meaning down deep in his spirit. From the band of mares and foals in their low condition, they had an elegance about them.

"We are tired, and you need to rest for your journey. I will provide for you guides that will safely take you back to your conveyance in the morning. Come with me and revive yourself to prepare for your return home to Cairo.' Looking back, he saw his new treasure following him. When she noticed his glance, she scampered away back to her mother.

"What a week this has been," Mike said to himself. Sissy was there at the paddock to greet him as he walked by on his return to the Sheykh's tent.

The sun glinted tiny rays in through the door of his tent gently waking him. He arose into what he thought was a wonderful dream. From his vantage, he could see Sissy munching contentedly. She must have sensed his stirring and lifted her eyes toward him. He could see the tribesmen scurrying around with their chores, but this morning was different. This was a vision from his childhood when he would dream of the desert and their magnificent Arabian horses. He was here in their presence, and it was really happening to him. He remembered the Sheykh saying to him that it is good to remember the horse of thy youth. In the doorway appeared the Sheykh's first man announcing that all preparations for their departure had been underway and his master requested his presence with him in his tent. He thanked God for these indelible moments. His focus turned to the task at hand. He was about to traverse the desert, for the first time, with this newly weaned filly being ponied beside his Sissy. His conversation with God then became intense as he asked Him for guidance, wisdom, and safety.

Entering Ammeri's tent, his familiar voice welcomed him. "I see you are ready Michael. Sit. Partake of the sustenance that has been prepared. You will need strength for the long trip ahead. I am an old man my son. I will not be accompanying you. We are all an integral part together in the co-creation of our horses with Allah. Journeying with you has been a highlight of my life. I know you are part of the plan as we continue our quest together. This is not finished. I will see you again, if not here, in the eternities. I will send you away with a blessing that Allah will be with you and you will return. I have something for you. I hold Walter in a special place in my heart as you will hold a similar place. Take this token, this copper bracelet for you personally. It will let the world know of the high honor we have for you. You will always be welcome in our tents. May your new treasure, RA Inshallah, grace your stables and bless your legacy with Shahwan. Your mare Shahwanyssa and you are one. It is not finished, Michael. *As-salam alayk*. Now go my son and may your journeys always lead you back to us."

CHAPTER 41

Mike's Safe Return

During our phone conversation, Mom began, "Son, Michael is okay. The story I just told you is incredible. He said the filly was not happy about leaving her mother, but Sissy did a good job of giving her solace in her distress, and she settled down in the three-day journey back to the truck and trailer. It was good to see him drive up. As his usual self, he exited the pickup and reassured me that just like he had driven so many miles and had gotten out of so many fixes, this one made the cake. He is beaming. I was wondering about the new filly at first. She needs a few groceries, but Mike comforted me saying that 'the horse of our dreams is only in the eye of the beholder. Give her time dear'. Something about Mike is different, his whole countenance has changed. I have faith in whatever he says."

I answered, "Thanks Mom for letting me know. I was worried, but somehow, I knew he would be okay. The prayers over here were going strong."

Mom continued, "We have been traveling to many venues with Dr. Marsufi. Both of them are spreading the word of the damage that is being done to the European industry by the spread of some American ideas into the Arabian show ring. They are talking to officials of all the Arabian registries in Europe and around the world. The World Arabian Horse Organization has even heard from them. Mike has been working with Al Aman's handlers and trainers in the philosophy he adheres to.

There has been a little friction from time to time, but Mike feels like progress is being made. The horses here are exquisite. Dr. Marsufi endeavors to place the finest bloodlines and individuals at the Stud. He is particularly interested in Shahwan and his get along with the addition of Shahwanyssa into his mare band. He has seen beautiful results. She has already had two foals. When Mike left for the desert, she had just weaned her second filly. She is such a great mother, Mathew. The Dr. does not want to see her leave. The addition of two fillies out of her has spread Shahwan's legacy to the Middle East. Mike is talking about returning to Alfalfa in the spring. The winter here is mild, but we have become accustomed to the weather. For the sake of the horses, we will return around May or June."

I commented, "I will be excited to finally have you guys back."

Mom added, "I can hardly wait to see how Josie, Philip, and your new baby are doing."

CHAPTER 42

Shahwan's Legacy

I felt a little something tugging at my shirt sleeve. This little bay colt had jolted me out of my deep meditation, chewing on everything he could get hold of. 'There is something about the outside of a horse that is good for the inside of a man'. I thought. The soft whiskers of the newborn and his aroma wafted through my nose as the colt investigated that thing in the middle of my face. 'Don't chew on your uncle', I would say. Momma circled and lay down on the warm straw. Her foal soon followed suit losing interest in my nose for the time being. I snuggled up with the gray mare, and we slept together.

Shirley peeked into the stall, whispering, "There is someone here to see you."

Mike opened the door of the stall with Mom close behind him. He looked at me with pride and whispered, "How is my treasure RA Inshallah, my Inny? And that precious little colt of hers? We finally did it, Mathew. Shahwan would be proud."

Inny looked up and saw Mike and cautiously arose. Noticing that her little one was still on the straw, she gingerly nuzzled the foal and nickered at Mike. Kneeling, Mike reached down and introduced himself to his long-awaited Shahwan son. With squinting eyes, the colt softly made a little squeak and then a whinny as he noticed his mom was not the one in front of him.

Jumping to his feet, he made his way over to her teats. Inny squealed with delight as he nudged her to stimulate the flow of milk. With motherly licks, she gave a bite to his croup, and he gave a little buck after she reminded him not to be so rough. Satisfied, looking up at Mike, with milk all over his little muzzle, "This is the fulfillment," Mike exclaimed, "He is gorgeous! Even at this age, I can see he is *asil*."

"I couldn't agree with you more. It has all been worth it," I replied.

Mike was home for a long break from his travels. Clinics and talks took up most of his time. I had agreed with him that I would be his base of operation in return for what he and Mom had done to get this clinic off the ground. I was happy to do it. My Miya was twenty-eight years old, and Kashahrah was thirty-two. The kids had already started their 4-H projects on them. Mike waited until the right time to breed Inny so he could be home with them when she foaled. He missed it by two days, but this colt was the realization of his dream to replace Shahwan. Creating a colt that would be able to bring his father's name and pedigree back. The Arabian industry had grown with breeders all over the world skillfully co-creating with God like the Bedouins in the desert. Mike was making a difference with his campaign to introduce his philosophy to the Arabian horse world.

Dazshtan, Shahwan's son is an image of his father. Mike will be working with Dazshtan as he did with his sister Shahwanyssa, who was now twenty years of age, using the same techniques and philosophy. She and her brother would hopefully join Mike to campaign with him as a team to show the horse world the results of Mike's program.

CHAPTER 43

Saving a Bloodline

There had been a communication from Sheykh R'Ammeri. It was requested that Walter and Dr. Marsufi travel to his camp where it was learned that the Sheykh had lost his treasured mare, the dam of RA Inshallah. During their return trip from the Wadi Sirhan, Walter and Rhaman discussed an honorable solution. On the phone with Mike, they explained the importance of maintaining her bloodline.

Mike requested that our family meet at the clinic in Tumalo to deal with an urgent situation. With us all assembled, Mike requested we join him at the stall of his beloved mare Inny and her colt Dazshtan. Somberly, Mike explained the reason for the important meeting. "I regret to inform you that the foundation mare of the Ruala tribe, the dam of Inny, has passed away. I have been in contact with Walter and Dr. Marsufi in Cairo. They have discussed a solution, that I also feel is honorable, as to how to preserve her bloodline," he noted. "Inny is in season. We all think she should be bred back to Shahwan to try for a filly. We need to return that precious filly back to the desert to replace her grandmother. What do you think, kids?"

Without hesitation, there was a cry of agreement from the family as a whole. I asked the pressing question, "Will the Sheykh live long enough to see the result?" I continued, "Isn't Walter awaiting an answer? We need to get busy, for sure. Right everyone?"

TO BE CONTINUED

Shahwan and Me in Aachen Germany 86'
PHOTO 1 CREDIT: MARCIA HANNA

Shahwan in Oregon 92'
PHOTO 2, CREDIT: MARY CORNELIUS PHOTOGRAPHY

Zalamero and Me undefeated 3 years after my epiphany 89'
PHOTO 3, CREDIT: UNKNOWN

Maria riding Shahwan fulfilling her dream 97'
PHOTO 4, CREDIT: INSIDE INTERNATIONAL

My inspiration for RA Inshallah. HMA Cazshablanca 2017'
PHOTO 5, CREDIT: CONNIE HUMPHREYS PHOTOGRAPHY

Walter Heuser. Who led me to Shahwan 89'

Margit Heuser and Jake 89'
PHOTO 6,7 DOMESTIC PHOTOS

Mokhtars Midnite Star after only seven hours of introduction to our world. From untouched to a secure and emotionally balanced partner. 2016'
PHOTO 8 CREDIT LEE ALEXANDER

Acknowledgments

RaNae Bangerter. For her graphic talents designing the book covers, title page and inside covers. Her ability to envision, teach, edit, support and guide me.

Lee Alexander. For her editing, inspiration, story consulting and imaginative guidance. For the experience I had introducing her untouched six-year-old rescued Arabian Stallion Mokhtars Midnite Star to our world, providing security along with the emotional balance needed between man and horse which inspired an important chapter in the book.

Janice Taylor. For her talented and wonderful artistry in capturing the essence and spirit of this work.

Gwendolyn Coley of Peach-Pit Georgia Equine therapy for her help in formatting when I needed it the most. Her moral support and kindred understanding of the philosophy espoused in this book.

Best Seller Publishing. For helping make my dream come true.

Dazshtan, Shahwan's Legacy

Book two in the trilogy

Made in the USA
Middletown, DE
31 October 2022

13817887R00136